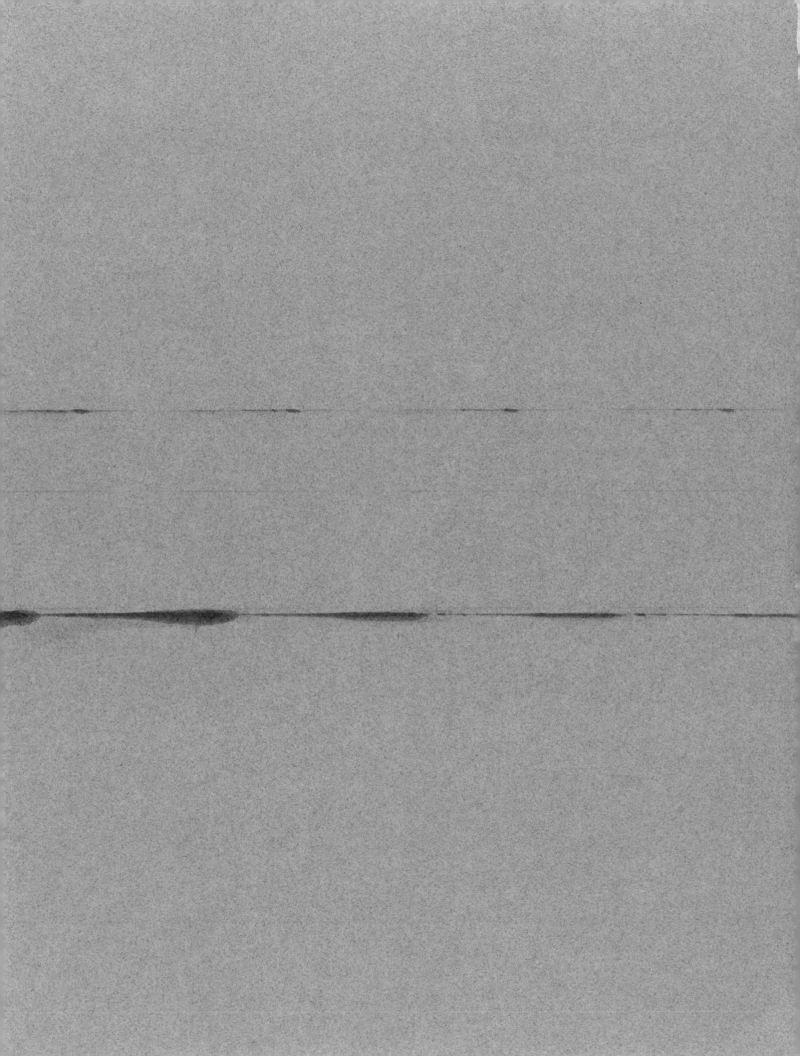

TRAPPIST

TRAPPIST

LIVING IN THE LAND OF DESIRE

BY

MICHAEL DOWNEY

PHOTOGRAPHY BY MICHAEL MAUNEY

PAULIST PRESS
NEW YORK/MAHWAH, N.J.

Library of Congress Cataloging-in-Publication Data

Downey, Michael.
    Trappist: living in the land of desire/ by Michael Downey.
        p.   cm.
    Includes bibliographical references.
    ISBN 0–8091–0491–1 (cloth: alk. paper)
    1. Abbey of Our Lady of Mepkin (Berkeley County, S.C.)
    2. Berkeley County (S.C.)—Church history—20th century.
    3. Trappists—Spiritual life. I. Title.
    BX2525.A33D69 1997
    271´.125075793—dc21   97–19977
                                            CIP

Published by Paulist Press
997 Macarthur Boulevard
Mahwah, New Jersey 07430

Printed and bound in the
United States of America

Contributors

About the Author

Michael Downey is Professor of Systematic Theology and Spirituality at Saint John's Seminary in Camarillo, California. Author of several books and numerous essays on Christian spirituality and worship, he is Founding North American Editor of *Spirituality*, an international journal of the Christian spiritual life, and Editor of the award-winning *New Dictionary of Catholic Spirituality*. His most recent book is *Understanding Christian Spirituality* (Paulist Press, 1997).

About the Photographer

Michael Mauney has been a freelance photographer in Chicago for many years. He has worked as a photojournalist for the *Charlotte Observer* and for *Fortune* and *People* magazines; he was a staff photographer for the weekly *Life* magazine. He currently undertakes numerous corporate photography assignments, with clients ranging from IBM to McDonald's to Rockwell International. Married with three grown daughters, he is dual-based in Chicago and North Carolina.

About the Designer

Edward Hughes is an internationally recognized independent graphic designer. His clients have included the Archdiocese of Chicago, The Art Institute of Chicago, Borg-Warner Corporation, The Boston Consulting Group, Chicago Symphony Orchestra, Huntington Library Press, Rand McNally & Company, and the University of Notre Dame. In addition, he teaches in the Publishing Program of the University of Chicago.

Contents

Foreword

Not often does a contemplative-monastic community seek to express itself to the world. Most of the time there is no need. For monastic life is an exercise in being, not speaking. It engages what is without only rarely, because it is caught up with God, who dwells within. But its eyes are always open to what is. Yet there are moments of disclosure. This book is one. Happily, the people who have produced it—the photographer, the designer, the publisher—have come to know something about us. But the author has looked at us with inquisitive eyes for a long time before he has spoken. By poetic thought and imaginative prose he has captured our life but with exquisite nuance, as a violinist would pick up a rare fiddle. He has plucked the full-throated string of monastic life, and the resonant wood has resounded.

This book is a world well beyond the normal one, accessible only by faith, not flight; penetrable by endurance not strength. May it become like its subject, ancient yet new, light but rich in your hands and mind and heart.

Francis Kline, O.C.S.O.
Abbot of Mepkin

Introduction

It is fitting that this book should appear as the Cistercians mark the nine hundredth anniversary of their foundation in 1098 at the New Monastery of Cîteaux. This is the story of the Cistercians, or Trappists as they are also known, just one expression of the great monastic tradition. It is the story of Trappist Cistercian life as it is lived in a particular place near South Carolina's grand old city of Charleston, the Abbey of Our Lady of Mepkin, which, in 1999, celebrates the fiftieth anniversary of its foundation.

Each Trappist monastery, every Cistercian house, has its own character, a unique personality, a distinct feel. But they all have a share in a common charism, a gift given by the Spirit of God, the Spirit of Christ, for the enrichment of the church and for the life of the world. Trappists live in a worldwide communion of faith, hope, and love. Each monastery is a school of charity. And so wherever they may live, the purpose of the Trappist Cistercians is the same: to become conformed to the person of Christ, united in communion with God and others in the presence and power of the Holy Spirit. This they do through a communal way of life that is disciplined, ordered for the purpose of constant and vigilant prayer, silence, simplicity, solitude, sacred reading, work, and worship.

This telling of the Trappist story is not the whole story, because the teller of the tale does not know the way in which Trappist life is lived today by all the men and the women in different monasteries throughout the world, let alone the way it has been lived in earlier ages. But I consider myself blessed in knowing many Cistercian monks and nuns in different parts of the world. The Trappist monastery with which I first became acquainted in any depth is the Abbaye Sainte Marie-du-Mont, or Mont-des-Cats, in the north of France. However, it is through my friendship with the monks of the Abbey of Our Lady of Gethsemani, especially Luke Armour, Matthew Kelty, Alfred McCartney, Patrick Hart, and Timothy Kelly, Abbot of Gethsemani, that I came to know something of this long and rich tradition "from the inside out," and have come to share in this gift to the church.

After the election of Francis Kline, monk of Gethsemani, as third Abbot of Mepkin in 1990, I was invited by him to visit the community and to give several conferences to the monks at Mepkin. Bonds of friendship developed quickly, and they have grown through frequent visits and through a deep and abiding prayerful communion over the years and across the miles. Nonetheless, the community's invitation to write this book came as a complete surprise to me, but one that I greeted with delight. To the monks of Mepkin, especially Francis Kline, I shall remain grateful beyond telling for the gift of their confidence in asking me to write this book, and in particular for the simple, encouraging words of two brothers, Paul Behr and Edward Shivell: "You're part of us. You know us—from the inside."

Many of the monks of Mepkin deserve a word of gratitude, but I would be remiss if I did not acknowledge Christian Carr, Callistus Crichlow, Stanislaus Gumula, Aelred Hagan, Richard McGuire, and Joshua Shlosberg for their continued assistance and support.

For her prayerful guidance and for her gracious assistance in my work with the Cistercian sources, I am deeply grateful to Cecilia Wilms, hermit.

When it was being decided that this book would be published by Paulist Press, I agreed on condition that I could once again have Kathleen Walsh as my editor. It is a pleasure to acknowledge the care she has taken with this work, as well as her finesse in handling an extraordinarily complex project.

The purpose of this book is twofold. First, it is to serve as a companion to the documentary video *Trappist*, which provides a look at Trappist Cistercian life at Mepkin. But this book is also intended to have a life of its own. Not every monk embodies the spirituality expressed in these pages, a fact that most would readily acknowledge. My intention here is not to provide a portrait of the ideal monk. It is rather to express the hope of what a monk aspires to be.

The work is divided into two parts. Part One, "The Monks at Mepkin," is written in light of several questions: What is Mepkin? What is a monk? Who are the monks at Mepkin? Where did they come from? How did they get to Mepkin? In Part Two, "The Heart of a Monk," I speak of those elements which lie at the heart of the monastic impulse. The sections of Part Two are written and arranged in light of the monastic and contemplative movement toward God. They are intended to move the reader to pray and to come to a greater recognition of the contemplative dimension of everyday living. The photographs appeal to the eye. The words of the text summon the ear. Through both, the heart of the reader is drawn into prayerful communion with the mystery of the living God.

Michael Edward Downey
Mepkin, 19 March 1997
Solemnity of Saint Joseph

Part One: The Monks at Mepkin

TRAPPIST

*Gethsemani made a foundation
in 1949 in South Carolina,
on a large old plantation
donated by Henry R. Luce
and Clare Boothe Luce.
Mepkin is one of the quietest
and most beautiful monasteries
of the Order. Still small and
practically unknown, it moves
peacefully along the way of a
Cistercian foundation that is
not in too big a hurry to
become enormous.*

Thomas Merton
Twentieth-century Cistercian
The Silent Life

Mepkin Abbey: Within a History

480   Benedict of Nursia, Father of Western monasticism. *Rule of Benedict* guides the life and development of Western Christian monasticism.

1098   Cistercian renewal of monastic life begins with the foundation of the "New Monastery" at Cîteaux in France.

1492   Columbus arrives in the New World.

1664   Cistercian life is reformed by Armand-Jean le Bouthillier de Rancé at the Abbey of La Trappe in France. Hence the name Trappist.

1681   Mepkin Plantation is established.

1762   Henry Laurens acquires Mepkin.

1775–1783 American Revolution.

1848   The Abbey of Our Lady of Gethsemani, the first enduring Trappist Cistercian Abbey in the United States, is founded near Bardstown, Kentucky.

1861–1865 Civil War.

1936   Mepkin is sold to Henry R. Luce and Clare Boothe Luce.

1949   The Abbey of Gethsemani founds the Monastery of the Immaculate Heart of Mary, later Our Lady of Mepkin Abbey, at the invitation of the Most Reverend Emmett Michael Walsh, Bishop of Charleston, and through the generosity of Mr. and Mrs. Luce. Twenty-nine founding monks arrive from Gethsemani on 14 November.

1950	The first religious profession takes place at Mepkin: Brother Laurence (Ferdinand) Hoevel on 26 February. The first Mass is celebrated in the "provisional church," the original church at Mepkin, on 3 June. Fraters Benjamin Clark and Linus Dodge are ordained to the deaconate on 14 January and to the priesthood on 3 June.
1955	The Trappist Cistercian foundation at Mepkin is raised to the status of abbey. Father Anthony Chassagne is elected first Abbot of Mepkin on 21 October. The solemn abbatial blessing of Dom Anthony takes place in Charleston's Cathedral of Saint John the Baptist on 15 December.
1970	Brother Paschal Harrod is the first monk to die and be buried at Mepkin (15 July).
1974	Dom Anthony resigns on 14 May. Father Christian Aidan Carr is appointed superior.
1977	Father Christian Aidan Carr is elected the second Abbot of Mepkin on 24 March.
1978	Brother Moses Weiner is the first founding monk to die and be buried at Mepkin (7 January).
1990	Father Francis Kline, monk of Gethsemani, is elected third Abbot of Mepkin on 21 January.
1992	The last Mass in the original church is celebrated on 22 March. The groundbreaking for the new Abbey Church takes place on 15 June.

1992   Mepkin accepts the paternity of the Trappist Cistercian
        nuns of the monastery of Esperanza in Esmeraldas,
        Ecuador, thereby pledging both spiritual and financial
        support for the Trappistines of Esmeraldas.

1993   The dedication of the Ecumenical Chapel takes place on
        22 March. The first Mass in the new Abbey Church is cele-
        brated on Palm Sunday. The new Abbey Church is dedicat-
        ed by the Most Reverend David B. Thompson, Bishop of
        Charleston, on 14 November.

1994   The Zimmer Organ is dedicated in the Abbey Church on 6
        March, and the Tower of the Seven Spirits is dedicated on
        23 October.

1998   The groundbreaking for the new library, infirmary, and
        commons takes place.

Mepkin: Origins

Mepkin. Thorough research yields neither the exact origin nor the precise meaning of the name. It is most likely an Indian word, since this land was once theirs. According to local conjecture, the name is probably the contraction of a word or words of the Native American people who once inhabited this "Low Country" of South Carolina. We are at a loss to recover the precise meaning of "Mepkin" because the dialects of the earliest inhabitants of this place have been irretrievably lost.

"Mepkin" might well mean "lovely" or "serene." These are fitting terms to describe this beautiful storied old property, situated on the placid Cooper River thirty-five miles north of South Carolina's legendary Charleston. The land is rich in pine woodlands and wetlands, graced with an abundance of ancient and majestic live oaks laced with gray Spanish moss sometimes drooping three, four, or five feet from their branches.

The ambiance and alluring charm of the Old South linger here. One approaches the venerable and secluded historic Carolina rice plantation by way of a stately, narrow, half-mile avenue. White Cherokee roses and multicolored azaleas border thickets of pine, yucca, Carolina jasmine, "elephant ears," and palmetto. Bamboo hedges the river's edge. Camellias and sasanquas brighten the undulating landscape in the wintry months. Spring's wisteria mixes with budding dogwoods. The look is like hung lace in lightest lavender, or tightly knit cobweb in lilac. In early morning and evening the deer brave the lawn on each side of the avenue. It is their place too, and they will not dart at the sight of the monk or the guest.

The Cooper River forms one of Mepkin's natural boundaries. Its tidal marshes, the twists and turns of its creeks and inlets, are home to

alligators, regal blue herons, water moccasins, and many other species. Frogs croak in strange harmony as evening falls. "Fish are jumpin'" from the waters of the tidal river, which, to those who have put down roots long, deep, and strong at its banks, seems to change a thousand times a day. This is just what the monks of Mepkin have done.

The origins of this captivating three-thousand-acre Cooper River plantation can be traced back over three hundred years. In 1681 Mepkin Plantation was established. From colonial times until the early 1900s, rice was grown on approximately six hundred acres called "Mepkin." Rice has not been grown commercially in South Carolina since the early part of the twentieth century, many of the rice fields having been destroyed by hurricanes.

This serene and splendid land was acquired in 1762, before the American Revolution, by the patriot Henry Laurens. Of French Huguenot origin, Henry Laurens was born at Charleston in 1724. A noted South Carolina statesman, he was President of the Continental Congress from 1777 to 1778. Because the Declaration of Independence was signed in 1776, Laurens is regarded by some historians as the first President of the United States. In 1781 he fell into the hands of the British and was imprisoned for a time in the Tower of London.

An avid botanist, Laurens established several innovative practices in horticulture and rice growing in Carolina's Low Country. He was renowned for his "Mepkin Plan" for the cultivation of rice fields along the Cooper, which was very successful and widely copied elsewhere. In the course of time, methods of rice growing were improved by Dutch specialists who had worked with rice cultivation and development in Indonesia, under Dutch rule until 1870. These specialists perfected the use of tidal rivers by constructing dikes with sluice gates, thus controlling the ingress and egress of the water, raising and lowering the gates.

After Laurens's time, Irish laborers, who came to the United States in droves as a result of the Irish potato famine, worked to improve the fields.

When Henry Laurens died at Mepkin in 1792, the plantation became the property of Henry Laurens, Jr., Laurens's sole surviving son. His other son, Col. John Laurens, had been killed in one of the last skirmishes of the American Revolution. A small cemetery on the property contains the remains of Henry Laurens, Sr., his family, and several generations of Laurenses.

Mepkin was owned by the Laurens family until 1851. For a considerable time it was abandoned as a plantation and residence, being used only as a hunting preserve. It changed owners repeatedly until 1936, when the large old plantation was purchased by Henry R. Luce, the philanthropist and publisher—most notably founder and publisher of *Time* and *Life* magazines—and his distinguished wife, the Honorable Clare Boothe Luce, a convert to Catholicism who was received into the church by the celebrated Fulton Sheen in 1947. One of the Luces' first acts was to commission the noted landscape architect, Loutrel Briggs, to create the Mepkin Gardens. Within the stately setting of majestic live oaks and the ever-flowing, ever-winding Cooper, he designed a terraced garden of camellias and azaleas second to none. It is with the Luces that we find the beginnings of the story of the monks at Mepkin. Who are the monks? How and why did they come to this serene and lovely land of Mepkin?

Monks: Within a History

The monastic community at Mepkin stands within a tradition that is centuries old. From the early days of the Christian tradition, some have

lived a solitary life in response to the call to seek God. If there is one thing about monastic life that stands out above all others, it is that monks are men and women who have gone apart to be alone, striving to be one with God. They have gone apart, often to secluded valleys or deserts, in order to give themselves to silence and prayer, seeking God in a single-hearted way. Those who feel the monastic impulse try to order the whole of their lives for the purpose of living in the deepest kind of communion with the mystery of the living God.

Monasticism is not unique to Christianity. There is a "monkish" element in most religions and cultures. Indeed, there is a "monkish" streak in people of different walks of life, even in those who have never visited a monastery or those who, having visited a monastery, would never consider embracing the monastic life in any formal way. Long before the emergence of Christianity, some people were inclined to seek God above all else, to find an environment in which their more solitary nature could flourish.

In the Christian tradition, the monk is a man or a woman who simply wants to follow Christ and to live the Christian life to the full in a particular manner. Monasticism is nothing more or less than living the gospel in a radical way. Monastic life is the life of the gospel, but it is radical gospel living with particular attention to Christ's hiddenness. The monastic life is an invitation to participate in the Paschal Mystery of Christ, with particular attention to Jesus' own call to solitude and his own discipline of going apart to quiet and desolate places in order to enter into prayerful communion with God, the one he called Father. About his hidden life at Nazareth little can be known for certain. It is not difficult to surmise, however, that as part of a pious Jewish family, Jesus gave himself to a regular discipline of prayer. What can be known with more certainty is that immediately after his baptism in the

The good zeal that monks should exercise with most fervent love: Hold each other in profound respect; bear patiently with each other's weakness; extend prompt obedience to each other. Pursue the other's good before one's own. Extend the charity of the brotherhood chastely. Fear God in love. Love the abbot with sincere and humble charity. Place nothing whatsoever before Christ. May he lead us all alike to eternal life.

Rule of Benedict
Chapter 72

Jordan, he went into the desert for a prolonged period of solitude, silence, and prayer. In the course of his ministry of preaching, teaching, and healing, he often went to an out-of-the-way place to pray.

The call of the Christian monk is to live at the heart of the Paschal Mystery through a life of silence, solitude, and prayer. The monk is caught up in the movement of Christ toward the Father, taken up by grace and drawn from present to future, from earth to heaven. To live in Christ is to be in communion with the Father by the presence and power of their Holy Spirit. Sometimes the monk lives alone. Sometimes the monk lives the single life with others in community. Whether lived alone or with others, the monk's vocation is to seek communion with all the living and the dead, through communion with the mystery of the living God. The monastic life, like all Christian life, is a journey to the Father in the Son through the Holy Spirit. In Christ, the one who lives alone is invited into the deepest kind of relationship—with self, others, God, as well as with the whole of creation.

The monk seeks the face of God. One embarks on the monastic way in order to seek God above all else. This is the heart of monastic life and calls for making this quest the governing concern of one's life. God and God alone is the central unifying reality of the monastic way. Monks embrace the discipline of celibacy so that they can freely center the entirety of their lives on the love of God and, by living in communion with God in Christ, grow in the love of others.

The monastic way invariably calls for the virtue of humility, a willingness to set aside one's own designs and ambitions for the sake of a greater good. This greater good is discerned through the teaching of a spiritual father, the abbot, or a spiritual mother, the abbess, and requires the spiritual discipline of obedience to the word and the will of abbot or abbess, who holds the place of Christ in the monastic community and

who earnestly seeks to make God's will known to the monks. Monks desire to know the will of God so as to be completely conformed to it.

Throughout Christian history monks have given themselves to the work of unceasing praise of God. The principal way in which they have done this has been to focus their lives on the Word of God in Scripture and in the celebration of the liturgy of the church, preeminently the Eucharist, the source and summit of the Christian life. From age to age, seven times daily, monks have gathered to say or sing together the psalms, the church's ancient language of prayer. Of these seven moments, Lauds and Vespers, Morning Prayer and Evening Prayer, are the high points of the monastic day. The great solemnities and feasts of the church crown the monastic year. The formal prayer of monks is expressive of a more profound disposition of constant prayer that is to permeate all their work and activities, indeed the entirety of their lives. The life of the monk is to be one great doxology, a continual act of praise and thanksgiving to God.

This constant living doxology is buoyed up by the monastic discipline of *lectio divina*, or sacred reading. This is central to monastic asceticism, the heart of the monk's discipline. *Lectio* is not simply reading; it is not scanning a page for useful information. *Lectio* is a disciplined receptivity to God's revelation, involving the continual, slow, careful pondering of the Word of God in Scripture. Contemplatively gazing at architecture, icons, or stained glass may also be a source of *lectio*. The monk may "read" an icon day by day, year by year. All creation is a book wide open and waiting to be read for those who have eyes to see. By *lectio* the Word lives in the heart and conforms the monk to the person of Christ. The monastic tradition stresses the importance of cultivating an attitude of receptivity, allowing God's Word to touch the depths of the heart. God's purifying

Word draws forth many things from the bottom of the human heart, but ultimately it evokes a loving desire for communion with the living God. This communion takes full form in contemplation, a way of perceiving and of being attentive to the presence of the living God whose name is above all names, but who is God toward us, for us, with us, and in us through Jesus the Christ.

In every expression of monastic life, silence and solitude have been emphasized. Monastic rules and customs that safeguard an ambience of silence are necessary in the monk's quest for God. Silence is a discipline that enables the monk to listen to God, to really hear the truth in the recesses of the human heart. Real communication is a rare gift. So much talk is insipid chatter or gossip. The monk learns that silence unites more deeply than speech, helps one to move from communication to communion.

Though it is a noble path, the monastic life is in so many ways quite ordinary. It calls for sinking into the mundane, the routine, and staying with it day after day. Most monasteries rely on an established daily routine that has been in place for many centuries. The schedule kept in a Trappist monastery today is more or less the same as the *horarium* observed in the Middle Ages. In the monastic round, there is very little change, diversion, or deviation. One of the monk's great temptations is to seek diversion, to remain unaware of the riches just beneath the surface of a sometimes grueling routine. The "sameness" of the life day by day can give rise to ennui and listlessness—what monks call *acedia*. The tendency, especially in this day and age, is to crave excitement, to look constantly for something entertaining. The monk's way is to take a step, and the next step, a small step each day, resting in the confidence that in due course God's promise will be fulfilled.

Monastic life is a way of asceticism, exercise, discipline. The monk seeks to become free of the competing desires of the heart, now for this, now for that, next for something else. Food and drink are taken in moderation as an expression of a whole way of life. In all matters, simplicity is the rule of thumb. The monk has a feel for the stark and the spare. Fasting, abstinence, and keeping vigil at night are disciplines embraced so as to stay alert, awake for the coming of God in Word and Spirit. Emptiness of body, heart, and hand is a manifestation of the monk's longing for the coming of God. Fasting is an attitude of the heart, the mark of a desire to be filled, completed. From age to age monks have waited, trusting that this way of self-sacrifice and self-emptying is a certain path of participation in the Paschal Mystery, and that by following in this way Christ is glorified.

Specifically Christian forms of monasticism began to take recognizable shape in the middle of the third century AD. Christianity started to accommodate itself to the prevailing secular society, and individual Christians became less critical of the values of the Roman Empire. Some of those who recognized the radical claim of the gospel on their lives, most notably in the Roman province of Egypt, other parts of Roman North Africa, and the countries in and around the Holy Land, began to leave the cities, moving away from the Roman Empire's centers of culture and society. They wanted to live the gospel in its fullness through a life of silence, solitude, discipline, and constant, vigilant prayer. They embraced this way of life more or less permanently. Some were hermits, living in complete solitude. The "laura" was home to others who lived alone but would come together from time to time. Still others lived in communities under a wise elder guide, a spiritual father or mother, an abbot or abbess. Pachomius (286–348) brought organization to this last group, the cenobites, who drew inspiration from the early Christian community described in the Acts of the Apostles. It is this communal expression of monasticism that has endured in most Western Christian monasteries today.

Basil of Caesarea, also known as Basil the Great (329–379), who drew up the monastic rules commonly used among Byzantine and Eastern Christians as well as some others, contributed to the movement of monasticism from desert to city. In part because of the influence of Athanasius's (297–373) *Life of Antony*, one of the great monastic fathers of Egypt (ca. 251–355), monasticism spread rapidly in the West. Different monastic fathers wrote rules to give direction to the life of their followers. It is the *Rule* of Benedict of Nursia (ca. 480–ca. 543), however, that became something of a model for Western monasticism, eventually gaining normative status through the influence of Charlemagne.

Monasteries spread throughout the Christian world and were found in a variety of locations, not just in deserts and out-of-the-way places. They were renowned as centers of peace and refuge, the focal points of culture and education. Little villages and sizable towns grew up near the monasteries, which soon played a crucial role in the people's religious and secular lives. As a result, monks gradually became more and more involved and invested in the affairs of church and society, and thus their way of life became less recognizable as a radical way of living the gospel. As monks became assimilated to the prevailing ethos of both church and society, some in their ranks called for a retrieval of the original monastic impulse, a reform of life so that it might be more in keeping with the call of the gospel in its original purity and simplicity.

One of the most important of the monastic reforms took place at the monastery of Cluny in Burgundy, France (founded in 909). Noted for its magnificent liturgical life, Cluny had a formative influence on

the monastic life of Western Christianity. A later renewal of monasticism that began in 1098 at Cîteaux, France, emphasized the solitude, simplicity, and true poverty characteristic of the earliest Christian approaches to the monastic life. The monks who began this renewal sought nothing other than a form of life ordered to the single-hearted pursuit of the gospel, which constitutes the core of Christ's call to discipleship. This renewal resulted in an expression of monastic life called "Cistercian," springing as it does from the source at Cîteaux.

The Cistercian founders—St. Robert of Molesme, St. Alberic, and St. Stephen Harding—went to a place off the beaten track to build a monastery, the "New Monastery" at Cîteaux, wherein the monastic ideals of poverty, humility, obedience, manual labor, withdrawal from the diversions of the world, liturgical worship, and sacred reading might be lived in their primitive purity and simplicity.

The monks at Mepkin are commonly called Trappists. The correct name of the Order to which they belong is the Order of Cistercians of the Strict (or Stricter) Observance, abbreviated O.C.S.O. Hence, they are more properly called Cistercians, but are also known as Reformed Cistercians or Trappist Cistercians. Their Order goes back to the renewal of monastic life at Cîteaux in 1098. The name "Trappist" comes from the Abbey of La Trappe in Normandy, France, where Armand-Jean le Bouthillier de Rancé (1626–1700), a man of deep pastoral sensibility, sought to reestablish a pristine, quite austere form of Cistercian life after it too had become moribund and insipid in its expression of the monastic spirit. The monastic life was suppressed by the French revolutionary government in 1791. Monks were forced either to disband or begin monastic foundations in countries where they would be safe. Notable among the monastic refugees was Augustin de Lestrange (1754–1827), the last novice master of La

Trappe, who led twenty-one monks to refuge in a dilapidated monastery in Valsainte, Switzerland. There they began a regime of extraordinary severity, far beyond the *Rule of Benedict*, and more rigorous than La Trappe. But many recruits came, and new monasteries were founded. Upon expulsion from Switzerland, Lestrange led his monks on a two-year pilgrimage, returning to La Trappe in 1815. There followed a period of great expansion. Within forty years there were twenty-three monasteries. The Abbey of Gethsemani in Kentucky, itself founded as a "daughter house" of the Abbey of Melleray in France in 1848, is the first enduring foundation in the United States springing from the efforts of de Rancé and Lestrange. Mepkin's roots lie in the Trappist Cistercian monastery at Gethsemani.

Monks Come to Mepkin

How did Mepkin, the home of Native American peoples, the home of slaves and Irish immigrant laborers who worked the rice plantation of Henry Laurens, the home of the celebrated Henry R. and Clare Boothe Luce, become home to a Roman Catholic community of monks?

In 1949, the Most Reverend Emmett Michael Walsh, Bishop of Charleston, received Mepkin as a gift from Henry R. and Clare Boothe Luce with the understanding that the property would be given to a religious community. Mrs. Luce knew of the Trappists through her familiarity with and appreciation of the writings of the Trappist author Thomas Merton, Gethsemani's most celebrated son. Bishop Walsh offered all the property he received from the Luces, over three thousand acres, to the Trappist Cistercian monks of the Abbey of Our Lady of Gethsemani in Kentucky for the purpose of founding a new monastery. The Gethsemani of post–World War II America was overflowing with

new vocations and was ready to found a new daughter house through the Luces' generous gift of land. The middle daughter Mepkin was founded during a period of great expansion in Gethsemani's history. First there was Holy Spirit in Conyers, Georgia (1944), and then Holy Trinity in Huntsville, Utah (1947). Further monastic foundations at Genesee, in Piffard, New York (1951), and Vina, California (1955), followed the foundation of the Monastery of the Immaculate Heart of Mary, now the Abbey of Our Lady of Mepkin, in 1949.

The foundation of Mepkin did not take place all at once. Indeed it might be more accurate to speak of three waves of founders. The first founders arrived in 1949, the second wave in 1952, and the third in 1955. On 14 November 1949, after several preliminary visits by a few monks from Gethsemani, twenty-nine Gethsemani monks arrived at the South Carolina tidewater plantation to establish a new community. Some of the first founders did not learn that they were being sent to South Carolina until the thirteenth of November, the day before their departure. A majority of the founders were still novices, quite unusual in recent monastic history. Among these founders, Brother Paul (Godfrey) Behr, Father Benjamin Clark, Brother Laurence (Ferdinand) Hoevel, Brother Gregory Krug, and Father Malachy Wall are still living at Mepkin. First founders Father Benedict Gemignani, Father Anthony Chassagne, Father Odilo Champagne, Brother Casimir Wiecki, Brother Conrad Greenia, and Brother Moses Weiner are buried at Mepkin. Some of the founders left monastic life at Mepkin to follow other paths. Especially noteworthy in the group of first founders who remained at Mepkin is Dom Anthony Chassagne (d. 9 October 1996), who led the community as founding superior (1949–1955) and first abbot (21 October 1955–14 May 1974).

What did the first wave of founders come upon when they arrived on 14 November 1949, after the long and grueling journey, some by bus, others by truck or station wagon, one by train, from Kentucky to South Carolina? They found a gardener's house at the entrance to the estate, a modern two-story edifice, several guest cottages, and other sorts of accommodation used for seasonal occupancy by Mepkin's previous owners. There was not much more. Now, as then, a good deal of the property is timberland.

Mepkin was not an immediate success. Economic strains and the severity of the summer climate posed real challenges to the nascent foundation. Several of the original group of twenty-nine left the community no doubt because of rugged living conditions and the intense summer heat. Mepkin's future was at times very uncertain in the early days. Thus Gethsemani sent a group of seven monks to offer assistance and bolster the strength of the fledgling monastic community. At the time, they were referred to as "the Seven Gifts of the Holy Spirit." Of this second wave of founders who arrived on 15 August 1952, Brothers Mary Joseph Szwcdo and Joseph (Cajetan) Lawrence remain at Mepkin. In 1955 a third wave arrived to offer further assistance to the young community. Brother Robert (Hyacinth) Wojciechowski, who remains at Mepkin, arrived on 19 October and was followed by a group of ten on 29 November, of whom Brothers Luke (Jeremias) Kirsch, Edward (Noel) Shivell, and William (Capistran) Slodowy remain.

Growth

In the almost fifty years of their history, the monks have truly made Mepkin their home, growing in spirit and in strength. In addition to the original church, they have constructed dormitories, a refectory

(dining room) and kitchen, administration and office buildings, a library and *scriptorium* (reading room), an infirmary, a visitors' center, a music building, and generous facilities for guests/retreatants. In addition, they have maintained the magnificent Luce Gardens.

Though not all of the buildings used for earning their livelihood are still standing or in full operation, over the years the brothers have put up twelve poultry houses, a small building for processing milk from Jersey cows, a machine shop and sheds, a sawmill, storage barns, and a "grading house" for processing and packaging eggs as well as for storing them in refrigeration. In addition the monks have built an irrigation system and have acquired a large supply of farming equipment and machinery. A towering aluminized water storage tank provides a breathtaking panorama of the region for the hearty and robust willing to climb its ladder.

Nearly two hundred acres of land have been cleared for cultivation. On these grounds the monks earn their own livelihood, providing for their own needs, for those of their many guests and retreatants, as well as for those of the poor in their neighborhood and in the wider church and world. Over the years Mepkin Abbey has passed on horticultural and agricultural traditions through raising cattle, hogs, chickens, corn, soybeans, wheat, azaleas, and camellias. In the early days of Mepkin Abbey, the monks earned income by selling baked goods, notably sticky cinnamon buns, which are still fresh in the memories of neighbors and Charlestonian shoppers. The monks of Mepkin have also been engaged in logging, selling the yield of their plentiful pinelands for saw timber and pulpwood.

The mainstay of the Abbey's economy today is the sale of eggs produced by a large flock of thirty-eight thousand Leghorn hens, which, on average, give just under thirty thousand eggs each day, or just over ten million a year. The hens themselves are sold in due course, making

their way into the bowls of those who slurp chicken noodle soup. In recent years, the monks have begun to utilize another rich resource that the hens provide. The production and sale of composted chicken manure is an experiment that expresses the genius of a vital and vigorous monastic tradition. *Earth Healer* is a blend of hen manure and kiln-dried white pine shavings, handsomely packaged and produced in accord with the values of the monastic tradition. *Earth Healer* unscreened garden compost, screened garden compost, and compost tea heal the earth in a natural and organic manner that is environmentally responsible and ecologically safe.

The monks of Mepkin have had to change and adapt their means of livelihood for different reasons over the course of the years, not least of all because of the weather. This serene and lovely setting is situated in a region that is visited by intense heat and humidity, torrential rains, severe hurricanes, tornadoes, and an occasional ice storm. Indeed an ice storm in 1961 resulted in the loss of rich resources of timber, causing the monks to explore new enterprises in securing their livelihood. In 1989, Hugo, the worst hurricane in recorded history to hit the continental United States, ripped through the center of Mepkin, causing untold damage to the chicken business, various buildings, and, perhaps most notably, the ancient and noble live oak trees. The major financial damage was Hugo's destruction of three-quarters of the timberland. The process of cleaning up after Hugo was long, costly, and arduous. Help came from several different quarters: neighbors, friends, and brothers from other monasteries. And like the majestic trees with trunks sometimes three feet in diameter, bruised and broken, the monks of Mepkin have continued to flourish in spite of periodic setbacks and interruptions.

Leadership at Mepkin

Perhaps the best way to understand the story of a monastery is by looking at its leadership. In a Trappist Cistercian monastery, the abbot, or
spiritual father of the community, is elected by all the monks who are
permanent members of the community, all those who have made
perpetual vows. A monastic community says a great deal about itself and
what it hopes to become in the election of its abbot. At Our Lady of
Mepkin there have been three abbots: Anthony Chassagne, Christian
Aidan Carr, and Francis Kline. Father Anthony Chassagne was sent by
Dom James Fox, the newly elected Abbot of Gethsemani, as founding
superior of the Monastery of the Immaculate Heart of Mary, Mepkin.
A Californian by birth, Father Anthony (born William on 11 August
1911) entered Gethsemani on 16 August 1941 and made his solemn pro-
fession there on 7 October 1946. Prior to his entrance at Gethsemani he
was ordained a priest on 8 December 1936 for the diocese of Monterey-
Fresno. As a diocesan priest he studied theology and philosophy at the
Gregorian University in Rome. While at Gethsemani he was a
professor of theology. He was also *censor librorum*, or publications exam-
iner, at Gethsemani. In both capacities at Gethsemani he became close
to the celebrated Thomas (Father Louis) Merton.

Arriving with the first founders in 1949, Father Anthony ministered
to the new community in South Carolina. When the new monastery
was raised to an abbey in 1955, Father Anthony was elected its first abbot.
During his years in office, Mepkin grew slowly but steadily. The land
was cultivated, buildings were constructed, and new recruits came. One
of the most difficult stretches of his years in office was the period following the Second Vatican Council, when there were many departures from
religious and monastic life. With the council's fresh vision of the church

as the People of God and its renewed emphasis on the universal call to holiness, many monks, religious, and clergy raised serious questions about the authenticity of their vocations and the integrity of their way of life. Many chose a different path, often at great personal cost and much to the dismay of their communities. Because of his solid theological foundation and his firm anchoring in Christian and monastic sources and traditions, Dom Anthony was able to lead the community through the turbulent times of the 1960s and early 1970s. He was a friend to many monasteries of the Order and a strong advocate of monastic renewal. Widely read in theology and related disciplines, he shared his ideas and opinions generously with many in the Order and well beyond. He resigned as abbot in 1974, in his twenty-fifth year of service in that capacity. After leaving office, he worked tirelessly at whatever tasks he was assigned in the community. In his service as librarian he was given ample opportunity to engage his love of learning and his continuing interest in monastic life and renewal. Ill health greatly reduced his strength over several years. One of his great joys during the final years of his life was Mepkin's acceptance of the "paternity" of the Trappistine monastery of Esperanza in Esmeraldas, Ecuador. Dom Anthony died at Mepkin on 9 October 1996, several days after a fall in his room.

It is impossible to summarize twenty-five years of service in a line or two, but two hallmarks stand out from Dom Anthony's years as abbot: growth and fidelity. Under his leadership Mepkin took root and sprouted. The early life of Mepkin was not smooth sailing. There were innumerable hurdles, but the small foundation flourished. This is due in no small measure to the witness of fidelity that Dom Anthony himself embodied. In the troublesome years following Vatican II, he was a stabilizing presence at Mepkin and was influential in the entire Order. His faithfulness endures and serves as a beacon to the brothers whom

he led to Mepkin and whom he served with great prudence and enthusiasm over many years.

With the formal resignation of Dom Anthony on 14 May 1974,
Father Aidan (later Christian) Carr was appointed by Dom Timothy
Kelly, Abbot of Gethsemani, as superior at Mepkin until a new abbot
could be elected. Having already served the community in various
other capacities, Father Aidan was elected abbot on 24 March 1977.
The second Abbot of Mepkin was born James Carr on 14 September
1914 in Galveston, Texas. In 1938 he entered the Conventual Franciscan
Friars and was ordained a priest on 13 January 1945. He earned a
doctorate in theology from the University of Montreal and a doctorate
in canon law from The Catholic University of America. As a Franciscan
he was a teacher, writer, counselor, administrator, parish priest, preach-
er, and editor. Most notably he served as seminary professor of theology and canon law before entering Mepkin on 31 October 1969.

Dom Aidan served as abbot until his seventy-fifth birthday and was
then appointed superior until the election of a new abbot on 21 January
1990. During his years in office the community continued the renewal
of monastic life in the spirit of Vatican II begun by Dom Anthony. Dom
Aidan had a keen sense of both the letter and the spirit of the law, and
his service as abbot will be remembered as a time in which the monastic
community was at once solidified and opened up. He sought to bring
the community to a deeper awareness of the distinctiveness of the
monastic and contemplative vocation and of its essential elements; he
guided the community in living the monastic charism in a changing
church and world. At the same time, perhaps because of the formative
influence of Franciscan spirituality in his life, Dom Aidan welcomed an
increasing number of monastic guests, as well as women retreatants, to
Mepkin. This rare combination of solidifying and opening up is the dis-

tinctive contribution of Dom Aidan to Mepkin. It lives on in the most generous and gracious hospitality characteristic of Mepkin, a hospitality that welcomes others to participate in the monastic rhythm of life while still preserving the integrity of the Trappist Cistercian charism embodied in the austere life of the monks at Mepkin.

Whereas the first two abbots of Mepkin were formed in the church prior to Vatican II, the third Abbot of Mepkin was educated during the Second Vatican Council and entered Gethsemani on 12 June 1972, while the spirit of the council was in full flower. Born Joseph Kline in Philadelphia on 21 December 1948, Father Francis was educated in Philadelphia archdiocesan schools before attending high school at the Jesuits' Saint Joseph's Prep in the same city. From there he went on to study music at the Juilliard School in New York City. After entering Gethsemani, he was sent to Rome to study at the Collegio Sant' Anselmo. Ordained a priest on 12 January 1986, he served the community at Gethsemani in various capacities, most notably as novice master. While he was novice master, Father Francis visited Mepkin in August 1989 to give a series of conferences to Cistercian monks in formation from different monasteries in the United States. Dom Timothy Kelly of Gethsemani arrived at Mepkin on 15 January 1990 to consult the community about the election of a new leader. The community decided to hold an election of a new abbot on 21 January. Francis Kline of Gethsemani was elected Abbot of Mepkin *in absentia* for a six-year term; he accepted by telephone later that day.

Dom Francis brings to the office of abbot a rich formation in monastic sources and the Cistercian patrimony as well as a deep love of the arts—music, fine art, architecture, and literature—preserved through the monastic tradition as well as through other traditions of

Western culture. Perhaps what is most distinctive of his abbatial leadership is a profound appreciation for the renewed vision of the church articulated in the documents of the Second Vatican Council. Under his guidance, the monks at Mepkin have grown in their awareness of themselves as a community related to the larger church around them. As a praying community within the church universal, the monastic church of Mepkin shares in the joys, the sorrows, and the mission of all the People of God to live and proclaim the gospel of Jesus Christ.

In 1992, during the abbatial ministry of Dom Francis, Mepkin accepted "paternity," or sponsorship, of the Trappistine monastery of Esperanza in Esmeraldas, Ecuador. This entails the integration of the community at Esmeraldas as full members of the Order through the pledge of Mepkin's spiritual and material support of the nuns there. It also signals Mepkin's coming-of-age, a maturity called forth through the acceptance of responsibility for a living and growing body beyond itself.

Elected for a second six-year term on 21 January 1996, through the grace of the Holy Spirit Dom Francis will, with seemingly boundless energy, guide the monks of Mepkin into the third millennium. While it is too early to pinpoint the hallmarks of his years in the abbatial office, it is clear that Francis Kline will continue to provide a fresh vision of the monastic life as one form of the Christian vocation which now must struggle to find its place alongside other expressions of Christian life.

In preparation for the fiftieth anniversary of the foundation of Mepkin (1999), and in anticipation of the new millennium, Dom Francis has led the community in planning for a new infirmary to meet the needs of Mepkin's elderly and infirm, a commons for the gathering of monks, as well as a new library to house Mepkin's splendid collection of theological works and monastic sources.

Mepkin Abbey Today

Monastic life at the Abbey of Our Lady of Mepkin is quite different today from the early days of the Monastery of the Immaculate Heart of Mary. The founders were mostly young and vigorous Americans, formed by the rigors of the strict Trappist life at Gethsemani. Today the thirty monks of Mepkin are of different ages and come from different socioeconomic and educational backgrounds. They come from different ethnic groups, races, language groups, and cultures. There are converts to Catholicism from Judaism and those who have come into full communion with the Catholic Church from different Christian traditions. Many have come to the monastery in their later years with plenty of life experience; others have come in their youth. This range of ages and backgrounds requires a great deal of creative fidelity on the part of those monks charged with the monastic formation of newcomers to the monastic life.

Indeed, one of the greatest challenges of life at Mepkin is to enter into the dynamics of fraternal communion with such a broad range of brothers. Before entering the community, one brother was a bottle washer, another served in the navy, yet another was a barber, and still another was a musician. One entered just after his seventeenth birthday, but most who enter today are in mid-life. This rich diversity is one of Mepkin's great blessings, but many in the community recognize the need for still greater diversity. Father Leonard Cunningham is an African American from Charleston who entered Mepkin as a Holy Ghost Father on 13 November 1960. While we were slicing loaves of bread for the community meal one afternoon, he looked at me and smiled ear to ear: "Wouldn't ya know it, Doc? It's the story of my life. All this white bread and not enough brown!"

Let there always be quiet, dark churches in which people can take refuge… Houses of God, filled with His silent presence. There, even when they do not know how to pray, at least they can be still and breathe easily.

Thomas Merton
Twentieth-century Cistercian
New Seeds of Contemplation

Not only is the face of the monastic community at Mepkin gradually changing; the place itself has grown and changed. One of the most significant developments at Mepkin has been the construction of the new Abbey Church. In 1989, before the arrival of hurricane Hugo and prior to the election of Dom Francis as abbot, the community began discussions concerning the renovation of the original church. In January 1991 the community took up the process with greater vigor. They chose Frank Kacmarcik for the project, with Theodore Butler as the architect. After consultation it was decided to change direction and proceed with the building of an entirely new structure.

The Mepkin Abbey Church is the first in importance of the many buildings that make up the monastery. It is "a house for the church of Mepkin," which has a distinctive personality and is a unique expression of Mepkin's style of liturgy and monastic hospitality. It expresses the identity of the community and its vision for the future. The monastic community is an *ecclesiola*, a little church, which finds its place within the *ecclesia*, the wider church, the church universal. Monks are part of the church, the People of God, and are called along with the wider church to full, conscious, and active participation in liturgy, especially the Eucharist, which is the source and summit of Christian life. The form of the Abbey Church follows its function: the centrality of the altar; the relation of choir stalls to altar; the relation of retreatants and guests to the monastic community; the placement of casual visitors; the creation of a smaller, more intimate space for reservation of the Blessed Sacrament and private prayer; the very location of the Abbey Church at the center of the monastic complex all bespeak a profound theology of monastic, ecclesial, Christian life.

The church combines enduring forms with the liturgical vision of the community in a way that evokes a particular aesthetic or ethos of the

monastic tradition. The building is almost barnlike in its utter simplicity; it is light and airy. In part this is because of its many glass doors, a
rarity in a monastic church. The vaulted ceiling made of southern yellow
pine beams adds height and grace to the building, endowing it with
extraordinary acoustical properties. The Zimmer Organ at Mepkin
Abbey is in the French Classic style, a combination instrument that
joins digital technology and pipes. It is ideal for a monastic community,
whose repertoire may range from very simple music to the complex. The
Abbey Church at Mepkin invites the enjoyment of contemplative
moments, indeed of prolonged contemplative experience, in and
through the beauty of the building itself. It is sheer poetry in light: pen-
etrating light at play with the simple, stark, and spare.

A more recent landmark at Mepkin Abbey is the Tower of the
Seven Spirits. This freestanding fifty-foot bell tower is the simplest of
forms. Its uniqueness lies in that it is a basic steel frame clad in copper
louvers, in a herringbone pattern. Its pointed cap, too, is of copper. Its
bells are from the Verdin Company in Cincinnati, the oldest extant
bell company in the United States. The four bells were cast in Holland
and are named for benefactors of Mepkin Abbey: John, Maria,
Bernard, Irene. The bells, which peal across the Cooper River as the
monks gather for prayer, evoke the voices of the seven spirits of the
Mepkin Plantation: the Native Americans who first walked the land;
Henry Laurens and his family; the slaves who worked the plantation;
the family of Henry R. and Clare Boothe Luce; the friends of Mepkin
who are buried on the grounds; the dead of the monastic community
now gone to glory; and the monastic community on the way, still living
at Mepkin.

Dom Anthony's conviction was that the contemplative, monastic
life is best lived with an eye to the history of the land on which it is

lived. The monks of Mepkin are aware of their call to be a sign of reconciliation and healing. The joys and sorrows of all those who have lived at Mepkin are taken up in the joys and sorrows of those now living, praying, and working at the Abbey of Our Lady of Mepkin. They share the joy and prosperity of the land of Laurens, but their life is also one of expiation for the sin of slavery, which was practiced with impunity on this plantation. And there is the untold pain of the earlier peoples, whose dialect is now extinct, the first inhabitants of this place that they named "Mepkin." Today this is the land of Brother Laurence and the other monks of Mepkin who live here amid their African American neighbors, being and building with them the Body of Christ both crucified and risen.

There is a story that lives on at Mepkin, one that provides insight into the soul of the community there. It was originally told by Brother Moses, a convert from Judaism and the first of the founders to be buried at Mepkin. He lies beneath the shade of one of the great and majestic live oaks, alongside the other monks of Mepkin who have gone to glory. The story is now told by Brother Boniface Schnitzbauer, a senior member of the community born in Würzburg, Germany, who, in his ninetieth year, still serves the community as baker and barber. While I was helping him empty the bread pans one morning, he told me Moses' joke in his still thickly German-accented English: "Those great big oak trees out there were once just little nuts that held their ground."

In this little cameo we see the lines of the story of the monks at Mepkin. They are planted here in this land. They are lovers of the place. Here they have grown strong, like a tree planted near fresh running water whose roots reach out invisibly but persistently to satisfy the thirst of the heart. Its shade offers a refuge of hospitality and forgiveness. The tree gives shelter to the great and the small, the robust and the weak, the first and the last. Its dripping Spanish moss encircles all who draw near, like God's abundant mercy. It too has leaves that have fallen to the ground and died: Paschal, Moses, Odilo, Benedict, Casimir, Gabriel, Conrad, Anthony. But the tree survives; indeed it is thriving, because its roots are long, deep, and strong. These roots spring from a little nut, the core, a heart awakened by the grace of Christ to leave everything so as to be rooted forever in the heart of God in a hidden land of love.

The Monastic Day at Mepkin Abbey

The day centers on prayer, work, and sacred reading.

3:00 A.M.	Rise
3:20	Vigils (Office of Psalms and Readings)
4:10	Meditation and *Lectio Divina* (Sacred Reading)
5:30	Lauds (Morning Prayer)
6:00	Breakfast
6:30	*Lectio Divina*
7:30	Eucharist followed by fifteen minutes for thanksgiving
8:15	Terce (Brief Prayer)—the Grand Silence ends
8:30–11:30	Work
12:00 NOON	Sext (Midday Prayer)
12:10	Dinner
12:50	None (Brief Prayer)
1:00–1:40	Optional Siesta
1:45–3:30	Work
5:00	Supper
6:00	Vespers (Evening Prayer)
6:30–7:30	Various individual and/or community activities
7:35	Compline (Closing Prayer)—the Grand Silence begins
8:00	Retire

Schedule for Sunday
Same as above, except the following:

7:30 A.M.	Terce followed by Eucharist
5:00 P.M.	Vespers (Evening Prayer)
5:30	Benediction
5:45	Supper

Part Two: The Heart of a Monk

That Land Called Desire

And God said to the soul:
　　"I desired you before the world began.
　　I desire you now
　　As you desire me.
　　And where the desires of two come together
　　There love is perfected."

Mechtild of Magdeburg
Thirteenth-century Cistercian
The Flowing Light of the Godhead

I s there more to life than meets the eye? If so, there is no proof. At least, no proof of the kind that so many of us demand. But there is a deeper kind of knowing, a knowing from the inside out, an awareness that there are levels of reality that are not immediately apparent. This is a kind of knowledge born of believing. It knows a different, deeper kind of truth beneath what can be proved by shallow, empirical ways of knowing. It comes in saying "Yes, I do believe." It is born in taking a risk and then resting in the confidence that the mystery at the heart of life and all living things is gracious and worth trusting. The one who says yes with full mind, full heart, full soul risks everything on the wager that this gracious mystery, the one believers call God, is more real than everything that meets the eye. This unfathomable and ineffable mystery—God—is worth living for. This is precisely what the monk does. The monk lives for God—or lives his life in the face of the question, Who is God? The monk searches out the answer through a whole way of life. He is a living quest for God.

It is not easy to define the monk. The reasons why someone is drawn to the monastic life are hard to pin down. There is no explaining just *why* one would spend a life in such a way: single, in solitude, living in community with others of very different temperaments, hidden, given to prayer and the constant search for the traces of God's presence. This way of life is marked by keeping vigil for the God who comes, who comes even now. But tomorrow the monk will again rise long before dawn to be found waiting for the constant coming of God.

Words cannot fully explain the reason for living this way. Many refer to it as a "call" or a "vocation." Monks strive to be conformed to the person of Christ, to be united in communion with God and

I have in me the desire to desire you and the love of loving you with all my heart and soul…. If we love anything, it is by love that we love; and it is by desire that we desire all that we desire.

William of St. Thierry
Twelfth-century Cistercian
On Contemplating God

others through the presence and power of the Holy Spirit. The monastic life is nothing more or less than living out the gospel of Jesus Christ, the same gospel that every baptized Christian is called to embrace. The monastic way is nothing other than the Christian life expressed in a particular way. It rests on an invitation from God. Like any invitation, it can be accepted or rejected, no constraints and no conditions; a simple yes or no will do. All those who say yes to God's call, whatever it may be, find deeper levels of freedom as they respond to it anew each day of their lives. God's call is heard differently in the life of each person—each call is unique. For some it comes in a moment; it is heard clearly, at once. For others it does not come once and for all, but gradually unfolds like a long echo throughout the course of a life. But however God's call is heard, the response to it is never an entirely accomplished fact. It takes a lifetime. Monks are part of a pilgrim people, the church. Monastic living is life on the way. It is a path to the heart of the Way who is the Truth and the Life.

Ears do not hear the calling. Nouns and verbs cannot adequately relay the message. God speaks, but rarely in full or coherent sentences. The voice of God hardly ever is found in complete paragraphs. The summons of God is heard in that place called desire: the human heart. Speaking of the heart is a way of naming the deepest part of ourselves, the center of freedom and responsibility. "Heart" is the name for desire, our openness to being touched by others, and by God. The heart is that in us which is toward and for the other. To have heart is to possess the capacity to be in relationship, to receive, to be touched, to be drawn into something more. "Heart" speaks of the human person's ability to relate to a world beyond the self, to recognize the claim of the other upon oneself. It is that in the person which moves toward the good, the true, the beautiful. The heart is the land of our longing, that place wherein we recognize what we want most of all. It is that space of the deepest wants, the ones that last, those that are more abiding than our passing fancy for this or that, now this one, now that one. The heart's deepest desire is what we live for, indeed what we might be willing to give everything for—even the one and only life we have to live.

The costliest of Valentine's Day cards cannot come close to expressing the language of the heart, the yearning of that land called desire. My heart bespeaks the unsearchable mystery of who I am before another, others, God. The heart is a place of freedom, of choosing, of being responsible. It is the name of my innermost self, who I am deep down, my true self without pretending, without masks, without cover. It is myself nude before the face of the Other.

The heart is a wide-open space wherein I glimpse God's gaze upon the contours of my own face before being born of my father's seed and my mother's womb. This face is gazed upon and loved. Cherished. But it is a face full of craving, longing, of wanting to be satisfied. Mine is a face searching the other—mother, father, others, the Other—always reaching out and ever looking beyond. Seeing and knowing, seen and known as God sees and knows me from the beginning. I am searching and stretching to know and be known, to love and be loved, to be free and to set others free. It is here in this land of yearning for more and yet more and even still more again, this geography of desire, that the Word of God evokes something in me, from me, for more than myself. In the beginning, from the start, on the first day, there is an "I." And I want. I desire. More. More than meets the eye. Throughout our lifetime this early, raw, sheer desire becomes more subtle. Through Word and Spirit it is purified

To be human is to walk around with God in your heart.

Francis Kline
Third Abbot of Mepkin

and thereby inclines to what is worthy of our desiring. In itself, desire is simply an indiscriminate wanting of it all. As it is gradually cleansed, the heart learns to long rightly. It comes to know what is good for it, what is worth wanting and having.

Because of the wounds it suffers from the very beginning, and because of the competing claims made upon it, every human heart is ever so vulnerable and fragile. So God addresses the heart through the language of mercy. All that has been done to me, all that I have done and failed to do, is embraced by God's forgiveness so strong and soft and tender that I just plain give in. I surrender. Mercy encircles the human heart, this region of wound, and makes of it a house of wisdom. The wounded heart is the place where the mystery of God seeks entry. Now. Each day. Every day. God wants in. Not tomorrow. Today. The monk says yes. He can't resist. He opens up, not at all certain of how it will work out. He desires nothing more than to be encircled by God's mercy, held and carried by the charity of his brothers in the monastery. The monk lets God take over his life. He wants to give himself up to God without reserve and with boundless confidence, committed to God alone in a community living by faith, in hope, through love.

The monk must learn how to sin, to be broken, to stand in need, so as to taste the mercy of God. His heart must be shattered and then mended. It thus becomes a map of Christ's mercy. Scars remain deeply engraved on it, making of the heart of the monk a testament to the unrestricted forgiveness of God still on offer to every human being.

The monk knows that God's claim on his life is absolute. There is no other. The press of God's mercy on his heart, the draw of the ineffable mystery of God's love, the desire to listen long and lovingly to the beating of the heart of God in silence and in solitude are all

The more a soul pours out its longing for God, the louder the sound of its voice in the ears of God's infinite spirit, for desire is the language of the soul.

Gregory the Great
From a commentary on Job

simply irresistible. He gives in to God freely. He gives the whole of himself, prostrates himself, lays down his life in love.

The monk seeks to enter into the relationship of Christ to God, the One he called Father. Through the mystery of the Incarnation, the monk is caught up in a movement with Christ toward the face of God, from earth to heaven, moving daily through the presence and power of their Spirit toward the promised future in which Christ will be all in all to the glory of God the Father.

Monasticism is a whole way of living in search of the face and the trace of the God who comes in Christ. Each day. All ways. But most often God comes in those we least expect: the poor and the weak and the wounded and the outcast. God comes in the "other," even in the enemy, those who have wounded this heart, harmed me. But God is also to be found in those "other" dimensions of myself, those forgotten and despised and rejected places of myself, that in myself which I abhor. Sin. Sinner. Guilt. Guilty. It is I and no other. Here I am Lord. Take me. Do with me whatever you will. I am ready for all. I accept all. Let only your will be done in me. I ask no more than this.

The monk knows that his call is none other than to live the fullness of life in Christ, the same fullness to which each Christian is called by the grace and Spirit given in baptism. He might have chosen to marry, to cherish one other above all the rest and bring up a family. He might have been a university professor or a nurse. Family and friends remind him that he could do so much good in a world plagued with misery and suffering. What good comes of a life spent hidden behind the walls of a monastery? Did not Christ command us to love our neighbors as ourselves? Why not *do* something with your life? What a waste! Prayers at three o'clock in the morning! What's the point? What good does that do?

If nothing else, life is a gift. And it is a task. We do not choose the life we have been given, at least not at the outset. Life is freely given. It is not of our own making. We do not choose the parents from whom our life springs, nor do we select the color of our hair or eyes or skin. Or a sister instead of a brother. Or the language and culture that shape us so deeply. In the same way we do not choose the call that springs from the heart of God, unique to each one willing to listen long enough to hear. It is altogether and utterly free, and, like any gift, God's call may be refused. It often is. But the monk accepts. He takes it in hand and trembles. The fear of the Lord is the beginning of wisdom.

There is no guarantee that he is doing the right thing. Many voices are quick to suggest that he is not. To make matters worse, God does not provide detailed instructions. Often God seems absent. Silent. The monk leans into the beating heart of God: "Speak, just one word!" Then with all the strength of his body and beyond it, he gives his life in its entirety into a whisper of fidelity.

Your Heart is a shrine that holds
An everlasting covenant;
Temple veil and Holy Place
Give Way, as dawn to morning light.

Cistercian Hymn

Wanting to Want God

The love of Christ should
come before all else.

Rule of Benedict
Chapter 4

What do you want? What do you yearn for so deeply you can taste it? The kind of wanting that governs you, takes over, drives you, makes you nearly crazy! The thing you live for. Well, it changes, no? First it's this and then it's something else. We want in degrees, and there are different kinds of wanting. Sometimes we want something so much we say: "It's to die for!" The wanting that wells up in us for morning coffee is of a very different sort from wanting to get into the best college or to see our children do well in school or our parents come through life-threatening illnesses. Or when we ache for the love of the one we love—that kind of wanting that makes you feel as if you are bleeding because it hurts so bad.

We want always and forever. The infant is a bundle of desire. New life is endless craving. But what we want changes. It all depends. What seemed a matter of life and death—we wanted it so badly—now appears insignificant, sometimes downright silly. We can't even remember what it was exactly that we wanted, or why we wanted it so much.

We live amidst clutter and cacophony. We want to have our cake and eat it too. Often our lives are driven and divided because of the many options available to us. We want to have it all. Everything. But the monk wants God, just God and God alone. Or at least wants to want God. He wants no more and no less. The monk wants with his whole mind, whole soul, whole heart. He wants it all too, but it is God that he wants. Or at least as much as there is to be had of God. If God can be had at all. If not had, possessed, then just a taste or a glimpse of God's face. He longs for a sense of God's nearness. There is no other reason for entering a monastery. Without wanting just this one thing, which indeed is not a thing at all, there is simply no point to losing the one and only life you have to live in such a way. The stakes are high.

If love is not whole-hearted, it is not whole.

Bernard of Clairvaux
Twelfth-century Cistercian
On the Song of Songs

God is not a thing, not even the biggest and best and most perfect thing imaginable. The name of God is: I am who I am; I will be who I will be. God cannot be tied down, cannot be held by our tightly knit concepts. If we think we have comprehended God, then what we have comprehended is certainly not God. The Christian claims "God is Love," but love is living, active, free. It cannot be contained. The monk's desire is fixed on this, but it is not a thing. And so the monk must be supple, malleable in wanting what he wants.

Desire grows. It flourishes. Desire in the wrong direction is deadly. It can take over our lives and the lives of others. It can kill. The desire for God moves in another direction. It becomes what it wants: good, true, beautiful. This pure desire for God does not want now this thing, now that one. Desire for God desires only its own increase. It wants to keep on wanting. The monk wants to be filled with the very wanting of God because what he wants is so utterly, ineffably good: to die for. God and God alone.

The claim of God on the monk's life is so complete and entire that all else is set aside—carefully considered plans, promising career, dreams of travel, the craving for all sorts of delights, the legitimate desire for security, and much more. But the taste for what has been set aside remains. The voice urging him to turn back never fades fully. There are gentle reminders of the successes and accomplishments that might have been his had he not left all to follow Christ. At times he forgets why he came to the monastery. At times he is altogether aware that he has failed in his vocation: to follow his passion, the Lord, the Christ. It is only the face of God for which the heart of the monk longs, God in Christ Jesus. Spending his one and only life in such a way is a waste if he does not get this part right. He spends his whole life trying to do so.

Some want to be priests, a worthy calling to be sure, but this is not the reason to enter a monastery. Others seek a life of interiority, a reflective life. This too is no good reason, in and of itself. Still others search for a life close to nature, attentive to the rhythms of the seasons. Yet others come to find a supportive community that might help them in a specific kind of work—study, writing, teaching or preaching; gardening or farming; singing or composing music. Some seek to escape to a safe and protective environment, betrayed and hurt in a world they think is going to hell in a handbasket. But the problems that riddle the world must still be faced in the monastery, for they are all there in the human heart. It is the region of conflicting desires, of wanting it both ways: now this, now that. Hearts are not left at the gate on entrance to the monastery. You bring yourself with you. Wherever you go, there you are. You do not change overnight. Envy, gossip, jealousy, hatred, smallness, and bitterness haunt the heart in any context, in every way of life. But so do God's grace and compassion.

It is the inescapable love of God gripping the heart that draws and keeps one in the monastic way. Becoming and remaining a monk are otherwise impossible. The monk is a human being like all the rest, with one crucial difference. The monk seeks God's own life with a single heart. He has fallen in love with God in Jesus Christ. Or at least he has begun to. The secret of his way of life is that he keeps on falling in love with God by giving himself day in and day out to the single-hearted pursuit of the one who is his passion and his peace: Jesus the Christ.

When we love, what we want more than anything else is to spend time with the one we love: to draw near, to get up close, to gaze upon the beloved, to be looked upon by those eyes, to draw from the breath of the other. We want to be filled with the life and love of the other.

Perhaps I have an obligation to preserve the stillness, the silence, the poverty, the virginal point of pure nothingness which is at the center of all other loves.

The Journals of Thomas Merton
Twentieth-century Cistercian

We yearn to be filled up so much that we cannot hold any more of it. And then by being filled to the breaking point we find that there is yet more room in us for having been broken by this love. Indeed, what we want is the whole life of the other. We want the beloved whole and entire. But we know that the only way to the heart of the beloved is by giving all the love and all the life we have to give—to the other of our loving. This is precisely how God loves. God's love and life, God's very self, is immutably and irretrievably given, once for all, in the person of Jesus the Christ, the very life and love of God, who is God for us. In this mystery of God become flesh we see what God wants. Jesus is God's desiring, God's loving, among us.

The monk catches a glimpse of Jesus. He looks at him and follows him, goes after him. In so doing he finds his own heart, and he gives it away again. And again finds his own heart in giving it away. To Christ, and through Christ to the others, every other. The monk wants to see the face of God. He longs for the person of Jesus Christ. Christ is the one for whom the monk lives. The monk wants to be near him, up close. He yearns to rest at the breast of Jesus, like the beloved disciple. To taste and to see.

The monk is a disciple of Christ Jesus. A disciple of Christ follows the lead of love in love. He searches out God in Christ because he has been left breathless by a mere glimpse of such goodness, such unsurpassable beauty, such clarity of truth. It is the truth of the gospel addressed to him, in and through the person of Jesus Christ. In the breathtaking encounter with Christ, the monk's heart turns toward God. He opens up. Now there is room, a place in him and in his heart for God. The very breath of God, God's breathing, God's Spirit, God's own life makes its way into his heart and soul. The claim is complete. Now he has no other life and wants no other life, than to live in Christ Jesus.

Monastic life is an exercise. It is a life of making ready, of preparing. It is constant training over the whole course of a lifetime. It is a way of toning up, homing in on what is worth wanting. It is a preparation for receiving what one desires—the one thing which, or who, is not a thing at all. The monk spends his life coming to know that wanting this or that can cloud the deeper wanting of just one thing: the One whose name is beyond all naming. "What do you seek?" asks the abbot. The monk responds: "The mercy of God...." He spends the rest of his life stretching to make enough room for the abundant mercy of God and the love of the brothers. His life is to be a witness to the wideness of God's mercy, which embraces us, all of us, even and especially the things we have done that can never be undone.

She held on to him,
yes, she held, and she held tight enough never to let go.
The more ardent was her seeking,
the tighter was her holding.
Happy was she in the seeking;
happier still in the holding.
She held him and would not let go,
she held on to him in faith.

The Life of Lutgard
Thirteenth-century Cistercian

Washed in the Word

"**O** Lord, Open my lips."
Response: *"And my mouth shall declare Your praise."*
"May the almighty and merciful Lord grant us a restful night."
Response: *"And a peaceful death."*

The monk lives between the lines, these two lines. He begins his day with the first line just after three o'clock in the morning. Before going to bed around eight in the evening, his last spoken words take the form of a prayer to God for the grace to die in peace. In that wide-open space which is his life between the lines, there is an emptiness in which God's Word might be heard. There is the Word beneath all words. It is this Word that the monk learns to listen to long and lovingly. But to do so, he must discern which of the many words he hears and speaks are expressions of the Word beneath the words.

Our words say something about who we are. They are a means of self-expression. In the Word, God expresses who God is. In Jesus Christ, God's Word, the divine life is immutably turned toward us, given to us. The God who is, is God for us.

We do not speak without breath. By it we live. God utters the Word in and through the divine breath, the Spirit of God. The Word spoken and the breath of life given are God's very self. God's own life is for us and for our salvation.

Each day the monk is washed in the Word. He is anointed in the divine breath breathed in God's speaking. He stands with feet sunk deeply in the clay of a community of faith and charity, the waters of the Word ebbing and flowing. They cleanse, soothe, chill, refresh, sometimes flood the soul. Over the course of a lifetime the monk comes to know the rhythms of the Word, learns the words of the Word by heart, lets his body shiver and sway and swoon at the very sound.

Seven times a day, the community gathers to say or sing the

psalms, the ancient prayer of the church. These words chart the geography of the human heart: love and loss, peace and conflict, rest and struggle, fidelity and betrayal, presence and absence, the gap between what we expect and what actually happens. In it all, the monk searches for traces of the presence and action of God. To give thanks and praise for what has been given. To be wrapped in the Word in good times and in bad.

During the night, while all creation sleeps soundly, the monk's lips open in anticipation. He keeps vigil. He is shrouded in darkness. He expects. He waits for the coming of the light. He wants to be filled with light, life, love. The unfolding of God's Word gives light. The monk inclines the ear of his heart to its subtle sound. The eye of his heart squints to catch its ray.

As morning breaks, the monk looks to God in wonder for the marvel of a new day. Faithful as the rising of the sun, God has once again made good on the promise. The heart of the monk is not abandoned, not left orphan. God's promise of presence is sure and constant. Count on it. The monk carries the Word of the promise throughout the day. Or it carries him, from the rising of the sun to its setting.

The day's labor is tiresome. Grass needs to be cut, meals prepared, dishes washed, sick brothers cared for, guests served, conflicts resolved, orders filled. And then there are the eggs to be gathered, sheep to be sheared, cows to be calved and milked, fruitcakes to be baked, cheese to be shipped. And the hands are fewer and fewer these days. Does it ever stop? It seems endless. Like the mercy of God—without end. A gentle reminder that wells up during each pause—at the third hour, the sixth hour, the ninth hour of the day—when the monk is sprinkled by that Word of God in the psalms. Like a balm for all the wounds on these calloused hands. Like a salve in the hurting places of this heart,

felt again as if for the first time today since the breaking of dawn.

As day dims, they gather again. The monks come together to bless and thank God for the gift of the day. They recognize what has been done and what has been left undone. They beg forgiveness for the harm done to others and for the good left undone. They acknowledge the many ways in which God has drawn near, especially in those ways least expected, even in the enemy.

God comes, most often in the simplest of ways: in an encouraging word from a brother, through an unexpected kindness from a stranger in the guesthouse, by way of a firm but gentle correction from the abbot. The monk recognizes the constant coming of God yet again at evening's coming. He has seen the light of this day. As it dims, he prepares to lie down to rest, to befriend the darkness of which is born the light: "Your Word is a lamp to my feet."

There is one last time. They gather in stillness to pray. They pray in the dark. Yet again the monk hears the Word, at day's end. Before going down to sleep he sends words to God: "Now, Master let your servant go in peace. Your Word has been fulfilled." He stands in darkness looking back on the day that has been given, and the one still to come on the other side of a sleep that will be too short.

Before closing his eyes, he fixes his gaze on Mary. It is she who gave birth to the Word. Mary, Mother of God, a woman enfolded in silence, whose silence now envelops him, each one of the monks, and us, all of us. It is she who carried the Word in her womb. She is his Mother, and ours.

The monk pledges himself to her, and he places his concerns, together with the hopes and dreams of his brothers gathered here with him and those who are away, at her side. They join their prayer with the prayer of the whole world. They ask for her help. They pray that

You don't have to read a great deal, but you should read deeply.

Christian Carr
Second Abbot of Mepkin

they might be faithful to the Word just as she was, with no guarantee of where it might lead. They ask the one who carried the Word in her own flesh for the grace of her prayers. They too want to bear the Word within so that they are filled with it, reshaped by it, as she was. Like her, they are carried by the Word into the darkness of the night and the promise of a new day.

Throughout his life the monk stretches to make enough room for silence. The peace and tranquillity of the monastery charm the guest or the casual visitor. Far from the clutches of the frenetic pace that drives many people in today's world, the monk seems soothed in stillness and serenity. His life appears free of interruption, cacophony, clutter. But monastic silence is not a haven from the hype and the harrowing ways of the outside world. Silence is a tone of being. It is a disposition of hospitality to the Word of God. The monk's life is ordered to hearing the Word, receiving it, guarding it, keeping it.

The ways of the Word differ. The Word is celebrated in the *opus Dei*, the work of God, the gathering seven times daily to pray the psalms, which are the church's language of prayer from long ago even until now. In this celebration of the Hours and in the Eucharist, the Word of God in the Scriptures is proclaimed and heard. In the monk's life, *lectio divina*, sacred reading, occupies the pivotal place. In stillness and in quiet, the monk attends to the holy book, God's Word: "Speak, Lord, Your servant is listening." Slow reading. Leisurely reading. This is altogether different from the kind of reading in which eyes skim the page grabbing quick and useful information. In *lectio* eyes behold, caress, embrace the text. Words are savored, chewed, swallowed, slowly. They taste of God. They are like honey in the mouth, gladdening the heart.

By slow and careful meditation on the Word, the monk lets God into him, lets God take him. *Lectio* does not come to a grinding halt

once the monk has given his hour at the dawning of day to sacred reading. Monastic life is itself a whole life of sacred reading. Living is *lectio*—a quiet and careful attentiveness to the Word discerned in the text of human life, in events, in the unfolding of history, in nature, in the ups and downs of human relationships, and even in the darkness of the human heart. The whole world, every inch and ounce of it, is a wide-open book. It is there for the reading. Pondering. But who has time? No one does. But the monk tries to make time.

The monk learns through the practice of *lectio* how to read the deep mystery at the heart of all the living. Most days he sits with a word, just one word from God's Word, and he listens. Long and lovingly. He hears again the whispering of fidelity: "Stay with me, read me, look at me, hear words of love from me. Write love to me with your life."

Reading the life of God long and lovingly by spending time with the Word lies at the very heart of the monastic discipline. Others, not monks, adopt a ministry of preaching. Some teach or conduct schools or nurse the sick. The monk lives a life of *lectio*. He knows that to read is to make love by taking care of the Word. To know how to read a book is a whole way of life.

There is the Word beneath all the words that clutter our lives. It is for this deep-down Word that the monk longs. To hear it he embraces a life of silence and solitude. It is a life of daily discipline. His is a life according to a rule, Benedict's *Rule*, which provides guidelines for brothers living together in faith and charity around an abbot, their father in faith. Benedict's first word to those who seek God in this way is "Listen!"

Wisdom is to be found in the monastery for those willing to listen. The monastic life is ordered and arranged for the service of charity. The life itself is formative. It makes an impression; it leaves a mark.

Just like a good book. Indeed, the monastery is a book, a text: Read, look, take it all in once you are taken by it. Here charity and faith are the lessons to be learned. This is a school of love. Those who would learn what the teacher has to say must pay attention. This is the first lesson. Be attentive! Keep your eye on that book which is written from the love among the brothers, working and praying, welcoming the guest, growing great in humility, being obedient to the Word of God as it comes in the teaching of the abbot and through the wisdom of a long life together with others in the school of charity.

One of the most important lessons for the monk to learn lies in knowing how not to know. This does not mean not knowing, but knowing how not to know. In this lies humility. Monks learn this in following a rule of life and through obedience to the abbot. The monk looks beyond himself. He listens to another because he knows how not to know. He does not stand alone. He can take all the wisdom the other has to give. He seeks profit from words well chosen and spoken in love.

The abbot holds the place of Christ in the monastic community. He gives his word and spends his life for the life of those who have been entrusted to him. The monk listens to him. Through the abbot, the monk learns of the mercy of Christ. The incarnation of mercy through the ways and words of the abbot takes different shape in response to the needs of each monk in the community. The abbot does not have all the answers. He is willing to learn from another even until he approaches the moment of drawing his last breath, because he knows how not to know. He is willing to listen, to learn. The abbot wants to make things loved by making them known. This he does by first learning how to listen to the Word, which is a language of mercy, beneath all the words.

The monk immerses himself in the silent waters of solitude because he knows that there is nothing more mysterious than words.

Sabbath Working

We earn our own living.
And we are satisfied with
that. We have a good
product worth the price.
But we earn to make a
living. We do not live to
make money. Choir comes
before cake. Prayer comes
before cheese, not to
mention fudge.

From a sermon of
Matthew Kelty
Monk of Gethsemani

When they live by the labor of their hands, as our fathers and the apostles did, then they are really monks.

Rule of Benedict
Chapter 48

Ora et labora, pray and work: These are the hallmarks of the monastic life. These two are the essential ingredients in the life of the monk, even though there is a bit more to it. The monastic life, in fact, stands on three legs. The first is the *opus Dei*, the work of God, principally the Liturgy of the Hours sung in common. This is the community's prayer at set times throughout the day. It is liturgical prayer, the prayer of the church, with the church, and for the church. The second is *lectio divina*, the constant prayerful reflection on the Sacred Scripture as the living Word of God. The third is work for the daily livelihood of the monastic community and of the poor.

The monk works six days a week, usually at manual labor, the gritty kind of work. On Sunday, even though there may still be chores to be done, he is free from work. It is the sabbath, the day of rest. This is the day set apart so that God may be praised and glorified unceasingly. The monk's sabbath day is Sunday, but the praise and glorification of God at the heart of the sabbath are to permeate each and every day. His labor is not just a job. It is sabbath working, day in and day out. He tries to be at rest and at worship even while working.

Six days of work; one day of rest and worship. Seven: a number richly laden with meaning. For the monk every day is to be the seventh day, a sabbath, a day on which God is praised and glorified. But in the Christian life, the sabbath is the first day, the Sunday. It is the day of a new creation, the creation of a new day. With it comes a new sense of time. Now each day is the day of prayer. The monk seeks to pray always and to glorify God in everything, not just on the sabbath. And not only seven times a day when they gather in the church to pray and sing the psalms, but here and now, whatever the day or the hour. Whatever the task to be done: "The kingdom of God is at hand." The coming of God is now, not then—when you get yourself to church with the others—but now. God comes even while one is mopping the kitchen floor or scouring the toilet, and especially when one is feeding the sick and tending to the elderly.

The monk is after the heart of Jesus the Christ. To love him means being like him, whole and entire, not just this or that piece or part of him. Jesus was poor. It was hard work he gave himself to. To love Jesus the Christ entails loving him in his poverty. To live in Christ is to embrace the human condition just as he did. It is no free and easy ride, being human. The monk is part of the human race; he is not above it. And tough work is not beneath him. He must carry his own weight and the weight of the brothers too, as Jesus took on the weight of his sisters and brothers, the wounded and the weak, the last and the least. His work is a lifelong labor of love.

There are bills to be paid and mouths to be fed. The roof needs fixing and the car cannot be driven without insurance. Medical bills have skyrocketed and the cost of heating the house is astronomical this year. The phone bill has gone through the roof, but people want to do business by phone these days. If the means of our livelihood is to keep growing, the phone seems to be the only way to go. And the fax. The computer needs to be "upgraded." Access to the Internet would provide useful information. More work, fewer hands, rising cost of living. Sound familiar? It has ever been thus, inside the monastery and outside its walls.

Providing for the poor and the needy in the neighborhood of the monastery and beyond is part and parcel of this way of life. In many monasteries there is a charitable fund through which the monks make provision for those who knock at their door asking for material assistance. It is not uncommon for a monk to establish strong bonds of friendship with neighbors and then come to their assistance in their infirmity, old age, or when they fall upon hard times.

Our works do not pass away, as they seem to do; rather they are scattered like temporal seeds of eternity.

Bernard of Clairvaux
On Conversion

The monastic community struggles to earn its daily bread, but the monk works for a different reason. Indeed he is to cultivate a disposition different from that which prevails outside the monastic enclosure. The work of his hands is not to be understood primarily as a product for consumers in a marketplace. Monastic work is participation in the creative activity of the living God, who sustains the world and all those in it at each and every moment. The fruits of the monk's labor are sold as a means of livelihood, but they are sold to persons, real people with deep needs, not bottom line consumers. Caution and care are taken at every turn, in marked contrast to the cutthroat competition that governs the marketplace. In the process of sabbath working, monks produce some of the best goods on the market! Whether it is cheese, bourbon fudge, creamy caramels, books, or beer, monastic goods are produced within a long-standing tradition of workers committed to simplicity, integrity, and quality.

The monastic understanding of work differs from prevailing views in the so-called real world. In the everyday lives of most people today, work is seen as a means of making money to do other things. Work is to be endured so that one can relax and enjoy life. For most, work is a burden; it is an out-and-out nuisance, a pain. Indeed, far too often people in different parts of the world are forced into labor that is back-breaking and spirit-sapping. It is downright cruel.

Even under the very best of circumstances work is often the enemy that robs us of energy, something to be finished so that we can get on with living. It's just a job. After work is done, we do what we really want to do, what we love to do. Like watch television! Or spend an evening with friends. Perhaps take some leisure time or do some exercise. "Quality time" is the time when we are free from work. Work drags us down. It knocks us out. As the latest bumper sticker puts it: A bad day at the beach is better than a great day at work. So many people spend the better part of their adult lives looking forward to retirement. And then what? More TV?

Though work in a monastery is often just as tedious as a job on the outside, the monk is, ideally, to be at rest even while at work. With his heart purified by God's presence and action, the monk does his work with the same disposition he brings to the sabbath. On six days he is sabbath working, since all of his labor is for the praise and glory of God. On Sunday and on the feast days when he is free from work, his worship is his work since in his resting he gives himself to the *opus Dei*, the work of God—lifting his mind and heart to God in thanks, praise, and supplication.

We want to do, to make, to shape, to give form, to give life, to pass it on, for the life of others and of the whole world. We want to love and be loved, to praise and give thanks for the gift of life, of light, of love. The human quest is a constant struggle for balance, for integration. For the monk, this is done in the milking of cows. In that simple activity, God is near. In gathering eggs, in weighing fruitcakes, in putting just the right measure of sugar in jelly, in baking bread, in wrapping cheese, God is to be found. Working and praying spring from one and the same source: the human heart. There are never enough hours in a day to get all the work done that is ours to do. And there are not enough lifetimes to thank God for the one and only life we have to live. There is no such thing as "job" or "prayer time" when ours is a life of sabbath working and laborious leisure. A human life is not made up of compartments. There are no pigeonholes large enough for the human spirit. It's all one, of a piece. Everything is related to everything else.

Happy are those who in all their labors and in all their ways seek blessed rest, always hastening, as the Apostle exhorts [Heb. 4:11], to enter into that rest.

Guerric of Igny
Twelfth-century Cistercian
Third Sermon for the Assumption

Work time, prayer time, all is God's time—the One who knows no limits of time. Any time will do. Look to God even and especially in this most unseemly task. God is so thoroughly involved with us and with all creation that if we could truly grasp this it would change the way we approach every moment of our lives. Blade of grass—just pick one—ray of sun, lazy lizard, cranky next door neighbor, the movement of the hand to help or hinder: all are manifestations of the living God.

Prayer takes many forms. Monks are called specifically to the contemplative life, a mode of being, a way of seeing. The contemplative is all eyes. Contemplation enables one to see things in perspective. Human life, nonhuman life, indeed the whole of creation is beautiful and good in its own right. The monk tries to see this. All is gift. Grace. Contemplation is the gaze that embraces without grasping, clutching, or clinging. The world and its goods are to be held and hallowed, even in their use. We are not primarily "users" of services rendered by "providers." We are not just consumers, but stewards, caring for all that has been given. Our responsibility is to let life continue, to let it flourish. The work of the monk is ordered to the same end as his prayer: that in all things God may be glorified, and Christ be all in all.

Living Alone

*We are more and more
forced to silence among
ourselves, but only that
we may converse all the
more freely and familiarly
with you alone.*

Isaac of Stella
Twelfth-century Cistercian
*A Second Sermon for the Fourth
Sunday after Epiphany*

The Trappist's solitary life reminds. It haunts. At times it hurts. The draw of solitude in his life is too deep to bring to words. We are born alone and we die alone. This is a simple fact to be faced eventually. The greater part of most of our lives is spent surrounded by other people. They encourage; they console; they challenge. Often they make us cringe. On balance, most human beings enjoy companionship, some measure of camaraderie. Most would rather be with others than be alone. For many, solitude, the single life, and aloneness are to be avoided. They are a curse. But the two singularly important moments of every life—being born and dying—are ineluctably solitary. We are single when we come into the world. We may be accompanied by others until we breathe our last and leave them and the world behind, but it is I who die, not the others. In dying, I am ultimately alone. There are no partners in death.

Created in God's image, a God whose very being is to be in relation, we come from others, live toward others and for others, and express and receive our identity in and through relationship with them. We are the persons we are because of our relationships with others. We are not autonomous, named and identified solely in terms of our own self. Nor are our name and identity determined solely by others. We are, rather, theonomous: our name and identity are from God, toward God, and for God, the One who lives eternally in a communion of loving relationship.

Though created for relationship, because made in the divine image, each one of us has a single, solitary heart. This is a mystery that is and always will be unavailable to another and others. The heart is the deepest truth of the self before God, that in myself which I seek to express in relationship with others. But the deepest part of myself—the fullness of the true self—is never fully available to the other. In the

most complete gift of the self that might be given to another, something cannot be given, no matter how much I might want to give myself completely. I am always left with something of myself that cannot cross over into another. I remain inescapably myself, and I am alone, especially in the depths of human pain and suffering. Even while living in the deepest kind of communion with God and all creation, with all the living and the dead, there is an "I." Until Christ is all in all.

Others make demands on us that seem never ending, and we often exact the same of them. We are surrounded by friends and family. We consider them a blessing, sometimes a curse, if we are fortunate to have them at all. We look forward to weddings and graduations, the weekend and summer vacation. There is always something next, something more to be realized. But it is often in that moment of silence, before giving way to sleep or just after waking, when the preoccupations of the day do not have the upper hand or when absolutely nothing is going on, that a wide space opens up in us: Alone. No one. Myself. God?

The monk has a taste for being alone. He does not avoid it. He is not antisocial but simply prefers his own company, relishing gobs of time to himself. In that wide-open space he is able to recognize the basic aloneness that is part of every human life.

The very thing that many others try to avoid at all costs, he embraces. He welcomes solitude, being alone. He knows that all of us at our depths are alone. He is called to the single life. But he lives this out alongside brothers in a community of faith and charity. Trappist life is life in community, but a community of a distinct kind in which the brothers are brought together and sustained by a bond of solitude and of silence.

The monk is celibate, and this is a daily challenge, if not a struggle. Unlike most other people, the Trappist is without spouse, family, or children. His parents don't quite understand why he would do such a

By the wonderful favor of God's loving care, in this solitude of ours we have the peace of solitude and yet we do not lack the consolation and comfort of holy companionship.

Guerric of Igny
Twelfth-century Cistercian
The Fourth Sermon for Advent

thing. Many of his friends are of like mind. His brothers and sisters sometimes share the same sentiment. Tucked away in a monastery? He has nothing. No power to change things. Little or no influence in the church or the world. Except the kind that comes by proclaiming the gospel with the silence of his life. Precisely the point!

There is not much support for a life like his. No one person cherishes him above all others. And no children to whom he has given life, in whom something of him will continue to live on, in whose accomplishments he might take great pride. There are not even some students in whose life he might make a difference in the way that schoolteachers or professors do. There is no one to prepare to go out and make the world a better place. This is the way he has chosen because he was chosen for it. He is alone, except for the Spirit of God in Christ and the faith, hope, and charity of his brothers.

He can fill up his day, indeed his whole life, with a glut of activities and preoccupations, avoiding the burdens and the delights of the single-hearted pursuit of God. There are always more things to be done. There are letters to be answered, phone calls to be returned, meals to be prepared, and guests to be greeted. There are always the opportunities for chitchat with other brothers in the cloister halls. Even prayer seven times a day provides a buffer against the truth: he is alone.

He may become fertile ground for the coming of the Word, the One for whom he longs. Or he may grow bitter and angry and frustrated because of all that he has set aside for the One he has never found, the One who has sought him but could not find him, so filled was he with everything and anything that might take his heart and mind off the fact that he has given it all up. Everything. He stands alone.

He may miss the point of living singly altogether: to be free and attentive and hospitable. He is to become utterly empty and altogether available so as to be found by God. And there is never more likely a moment than when he is quiet enough, still enough, empty enough. The hollow spaces in him are the very places where he might be completely available to the One for whom he searches, on whose coming he waits.

In his waiting, in his living alone, the whisper and the wonder well up within him. His prayer rises to God: "Is it long enough? This waiting. How much longer? How much more? This emptiness. The loneliness, this wanting something to touch, to assure. One word. Speak just one word! And I shall hold on, hold out, longer still. There is no other. No other one but You. It is You I seek. It is You alone for whom I ache, hurt, wounded in wanting to make room for You. In your visitation you do not come alone, but bring the others with you. All. The others. You do not dwell in heavenly solitary bliss, but live in a communion of persons. In all. In the others. It is You for whom I have waited and will wait until eternal morning breaks. You who are nearer than I am to my own self—not a self—but in communion. In loving communion, I live. No longer I."

Welcoming the Other

And you too, the friend of
my final moment, who
would not have known
what you are doing. Yes,
I also say THANK YOU and
A-DIEU to you, in whom
I see the face of God.

Christian de Chergé
Cistercian Prior
of Our Lady of Atlas.

From a testament written during
Advent 1993 in view of the threat
of murder by Algerian terrorists.
Dom Christian and six of the monks
of Atlas were murdered by terrorists
on 21 May 1996.

The monastery is not a place to "get away from it all." It is rather the place for getting out of the way. The monastic life is an environment wherein one faces the self and puts the self aside. In the monastic way the self is decentered. The monastic life entails the lifelong task of making room for the other: another, others, God. It is a space for welcoming the other, a center of hospitality. Hospitality is openness to the unknown, expending the self on the unfamiliar, the stranger, the exile. The monk is called to sustained hospitality to the guest and the stranger both within and outside the community. He does not live for himself but is toward and for the other, toward that which lies beyond himself and his own immediate concerns.

Monks are homemakers. They create homes for the cultivation of relationships of a specific kind: founded and flourishing in charity. The monk is to make room for those who are different from himself— even for the enemy, recognizing the face of God even and especially there.

Ours is a culture of individual rights and liberties. Nothing seems to be valued so highly as the freedom of choice and self-determination. Our heroes and heroines are those who stand on their own two feet no matter what the cost, whose solo anthem defies harmonization: "I did it my way." The American dream comes true when we pull ourselves up by our own bootstraps, when we can make it on our own—come hell or high water. But far too often the individual's accomplishment is at the expense of others along the way as one climbs the ladder of success. Or of survival. From the time of early childhood on, the message is deeply ingrained: God helps those who help themselves. It is then an easy step to its correlate: "It's every man for himself."

The monk lives no longer for himself but for God in Christ. God's providential plan for him is discerned not in flying solo but in throwing in his lot with his brothers and searching out their common good. While the monk is one who lives alone by most standards, he is inescapably a team player. His life is not his own. But even those with whom he lives remain strangers, mysteries, always other than himself. And they are always making a claim on him.

Monastic life includes a call to move away gradually from self-preoccupation, self-absorption, self-fixation. The monastery is a field on which selfishness is the target of frontal assault. People in other walks of life face the demon of narcissism as they struggle with balancing self-interest with the care and service of children, spouse, aging parents, students, or coworkers. In the monastery, individual needs and wants must be negotiated in light of the common will of the community as expressed in traditions, communal decisions, and the teaching and the counsel of the abbot.

The monastic life involves a constant surrender to that which is other and unknown. Above all the monk surrenders to the Other of God, the ineffable, who will not be tamed, domesticated, or controlled. God is that Other who makes a radical claim on my life—precisely as Other.

The monk searches for the face of the Other of God precisely as other. God is elusive, always more, overspilling our concepts. Decentering the self, making room for the Other of God through humility and obedience, entails the discipline of hospitality. It means making room in oneself for all who challenge us to move beyond the narrow confines of self-absorption, self-fixation, self-preoccupation. Through constant hospitality the monk is able to make room for the other: the other person, other people, and the Other who is God. Solitude makes it possible to share in the things that really matter. This is expressed particularly in hospitality toward guests and strangers, and in caring for the infirm and the aged, the wounded and the weak, the last and the least in the community. It also entails making room in the self for the common good, the common will, as it is discerned through the wisdom of the brothers and the teaching of the abbot.

On the surface, the monastery is a peaceful, tranquil place. Indeed it is a domestic place: cooking, gardening, washing, tending to the needs of the brothers, praying. But to be a monk is to entertain the stranger, the exile, the other precisely as an other, one's whole life long. It involves getting out of the way so that the other can live precisely as other than myself.

It is no easy matter to make room in a life for others. Each makes a claim, asks for something: time, energy, resources, commitment. Even if we are reluctant to do so, we usually surrender to the others in our lives, gradually learning to sift through the claims they make on us. There are children to be fed and clothed, students to be taught, deadlines to be met. But far too often in our relationships with others we perceive them as mere extensions of ourselves: children, parents, friends, colleagues, coworkers, community members, parishioners. We relate to them, indeed comply with the claims they make on us, because in so doing there is something in it for us. But it is an altogether different matter to submit to the claim of another precisely as other. There is an other whose otherness is radically different from myself. The other has a right to ask something of me, wants to know where I stand, and asks that I respond to a need. The other is a person, not just an extension of myself. The other has a face, and it is often not very pretty. The other has a name, and it is not mine.

Here lies the core of monastic asceticism. Welcoming the other as other is the very heart of the discipline of a monastery. To stand in one

place, to put down lasting roots with others, and to respond to the claim of the other as an other, not as an appendage of my own always-too-small self. Above all it is the Other of God in Christ who makes the most radical claim on the monk, who demands everything. But this claim is manifest in the claims of others encountered day by day, most often in the least likely places and persons—the monk's brothers and beyond them—and in the least likely regions of the deepest self, wounded and weak, vulnerable and volatile. Is there really room enough in our lives for the other we would rather let remain other—the stranger, the exile?

Not every claim that the other makes on me is legitimate, and so there is the need for constant discernment, sifting through, sorting out the true from the false, that which is of God from that which comes from elsewhere. Other forces divide, turn one against the other with the allure of independence, self-sufficiency, and self-actualization. And so the monk submits to the other of the abbot, whose teaching and whose wisdom may help in the ways of light, life, and love.

The abbot holds the place of Christ in the community. But Christ does not stand alone. He is what he is in and through loving relationship with the Father in the Spirit. Likewise the abbot does not stand alone. He is not above reproach or correction. He is the father of many brothers who live and breathe by the Holy Spirit who has been poured into their hearts. The abbot is responsible for the monks' life and growth in faith and charity, for the flourishing of the gifts of the Holy Spirit in each one, just as they are responsible to him. They make a claim on him, precisely as others with their own needs and demands, their own smallness and largesse of heart. The abbot looks to them, searches for the shared wisdom to be found in their common life, giving it back to them, to the others, for their life of grace and for the life of the world. He too is visited by the other, the Father Immediate, abbot of the motherhouse, who may make demands or require that he change or urge him to be more supple in the ways of the Spirit, more subtle in the way that he directs the community.

Making room to welcome the other demands the recognition that we are not the center of the universe. It is not all about us, though at times we would like it to be. Monastic life is a relentless process of de-selfing, de-egoization. It is first and finally about humility. The monastery is the place where the self is at once defined and dissolved. The monk is nothing more than one of the brothers, even when he holds the place of Christ among them as abbot; for it is the Christ of the *kenosis*, the Lord of self-emptying love, in whose place he stands. He holds the place of the one whose power is known in the washing of feet, in service, in self-sacrificial love, in laying down his life, in relinquishing any claim to lordship. His only hope is in God's promise of presence. His only love is the love of not having, so that there is room enough for the Other of God. And for every other who comes his way and claims the one and only life he has to give.

Hospitality is one of the hallmarks of the monastery. Benedict instructs monks: "Let all guests be received as Christ." This involves making provision for the material and spiritual needs of the many guests who pass through for a casual visit, for a retreat, or for a prolonged stay at the monastery. At times the monastery is a refuge for those in desperate need, especially the sinner in search of the unrestricted forgiveness and mercy about which the monks sing. It is a sanctuary. There is no red carpet. Yet there is an open door there. At least there is that. A space of peace and bread and bed, encircled in prayer and praise. Each is received as Christ with openness and

generosity because of the inherent dignity carried in the heart of each one, no matter how bruised the spirit may be. But Christ is not just to be fed and clothed and housed.

Listen. Watch. Attend. Wait. Receive. Welcome. This other is as Christ among you, in your midst, under your roof. O Lord, am I worthy?

Monks make room, enough room for the other. This is a task that is never entirely accomplished. It involves following a path of downward mobility rather than racing along the superhighway of the never-ending "upgrade." The monk's task is to relinquish rather than acquire so that there is room, space, for the Other beyond the clutter and the noise with which we are filled. Monastic asceticism, discipline, is aimed at renouncing any claim to control the other so that I might truly know the other and the claim of the other on me. And through this emptying of the self that claims to be the center of the universe, to have room enough so that the supremely Other might make a claim on me and be all in all.

The monk is one who through the discipline of humility and hiddenness abandons himself as an individual self and enters the paradise of communion through community. His life is one of stripping himself of all he knows and understands, a disciplined waiting for the arrival of the other, allowing others to be in all their strangeness. Monastic life writes into the body of the monk the process of impoverishment, of descent into darkness, of unknowing, of not-having.

The monk lives, writes, his life alone in communion. His call is to trace his life out in silence. He tries to get out of the way, so that there might be room for more. His life's work is to make room for the God who comes as Other in the other. Every other.

Living in Communion

So embrace the whole world with the arms of your love and in
*   that act at once consider and congratulate the good,*
*   contemplate and mourn over the wicked.*
In that act look upon the afflicted and the oppressed and
*   feel compassion for them.*
In that act call to mind the wretchedness of the poor, the
*   groans of orphans, the abandonment of widows, the gloom*
*   of the sorrowful, the needs of travellers, the prayers*
*   of virgins, the perils of those at sea, the temptations*
*   of monks, the responsibilities of prelates, the labors*
*   of those waging war.*
In your love take them all to your heart, weep over them,
*   offer your prayers for them.*

Aelred of Rievaulx
Twelfth-century Cistercian
A Rule of Life for a Recluse

I t is a life of silence and solitude. It is also life in community, living up close. The monastic life demands that the monk throw his lot in with others he might not have chosen as his friends. He may have little affinity for the tastes and temperaments of his brothers. Living under the same roof are men from very different walks of life. Their backgrounds differ. The same monastery may include brothers of different races and languages. Each has his own story. The Trappist may withdraw from the world and from ordinary occupations, but he brings it all with him into the monastic enclosure. Monastic life is human life. And because it is life up close with persons who have not chosen one another as friends or lovers, it is like living in a pressure cooker—with the heat turned up to full blast!

A shared sense of meaning, value, purpose is what binds these very different people together in community, seeking the face of the living God. Community life is not an end in itself nor the primary reason for joining the monastery. Community is an expression of communion, that mystery at the heart of the world and of all the living in which everything is related to everything else. Living in community is no guarantee of living in the mystery of communion. Some who live alone and in utter isolation may in fact participate more fully in the mystery of communion than some who are surrounded by the presence and the company of others. But the monk's way is in and through community as an expression of this deep and abiding communion.

The monastery offers an invitation to the deepest kind of communion by schooling its members in the ways of charity. Indeed the monastery is to be a school of charity; it is a house of self-sacrificial love. The brothers lay down their lives for one another. They pledge themselves to one another, to love this place, to stay rooted in it alongside one another, until death. They are to be lovers of their

Nothing in life is happier than to love faithfully and to be loved in return.

From a letter of Adam of Perseigne
Thirteenth-century Cistercian

brothers, and lovers of the place: this monastery, this house of prayer, this school of love.

Silence and solitude allow for a particular way of living in community. Though the brothers live up close to one another, a common commitment to the discipline of silence and a profound respect for the solitude of each one holds them together. Most of every day is spent in the company of the other monks: frugal meals in silence are shared at a common table; most of the day's work is done together with the other brothers; they gather for prayer seven times a day; sleeping quarters are sometimes a bit small. The common life of the brothers is not to be a distraction along the way to living in the fullness of the divine life; the community is not an obstacle to be hurdled. The common life itself conforms the monk to the person of Christ, particularly in the mystery of his hiddenness and obscurity.

The whole of the monastic life is ordered to the search for God in prayer. But God is not a self-contained Being unrelated to human beings or to the world. The Trinity is the uniquely Christian way of naming the mystery of God as a communion of persons in loving and eternal relation—Father, Son, Spirit. In the Christian vision, it is inconceivable that there was ever a moment when God was not in relation. God did not exist as a self-sufficient One who only later decides to speak the Word and breathe the Spirit. It is God's very nature to be in loving relationship: Father, Son, and Spirit with one another, for us, with us, in us. The monk gives himself over so that he may be swept up in this interaction. He seeks to live at the heart of the mystery of communion.

To be created in God's image is to be created with the capacity to be in relationship with self, another, others, and God. Finding our true selves means being conformed to the person of Christ, being united in

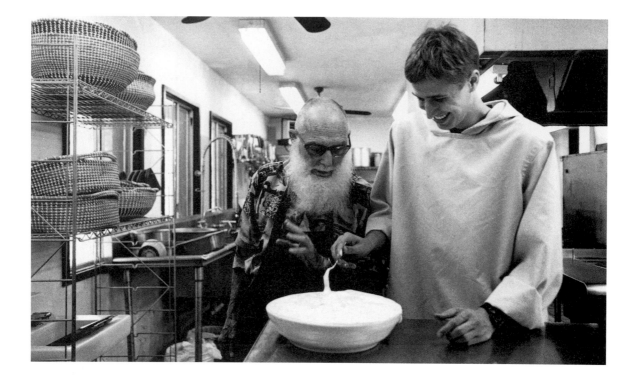

communion with God and others. The deepest desire of the human
heart is for relationship, for living the fullness of communion. When
we taste this communion, we come to know—at times slowly and
ploddingly while at other times in a moment of dazzling darkness—
that relationship is the deepest and fullest of the divine mysteries.
Everything is related to everything else. It all hangs together because
everything that exists participates in the life of the living God, whose
very nature is to be in relation.

All of creation breathes by the presence and power of the living
God. Telltale hints of the divine breath exist everywhere, but most of
all in the loving communion of human persons in relationship. Not all
human relationships bespeak the presence of the living God; our ways
of relating can be suffocating and death-dealing. But relationships of
mutuality, equality, and reciprocity mirror the very life of Father, Son,
and Spirit. Herein we catch the clearest glimpse of the vestiges of the
living God. We are created in the image of a God who lives in
communion. Living in this communion of persons, divine and human,
is our destiny. It is the meaning of salvation. The full participation of
all the living in this communion of persons is God's providential plan
for all humanity.

The monk participates in the mystery of communion preeminently
through the common life with his brothers. All his work, prayer, and
worship are ordered to fuller participation in this mystery of
communion. The life of the mind is cultivated through *lectio divina*
and through study. The purpose of *lectio* and study in the monastic life
is not to gather useful information about the Scriptures or the Patristic
sources or the great spiritual guides of the church, East and West.
Rather, through *lectio* and study the monk participates in the very life
of God. The reflective life in the monastic tradition is an activity by

which God is glorified. Study is an act of praise: the better known, the more God is loved and adored. Contemplation does not lie primarily in the undisturbed mind's pure gaze upon eternal, unchanging truth—up there or out there. It is more a matter of seeing the ordinary and the everyday as the arena of God's presence and action. God is to be found in the rigorous sacrifices entailed in caring for the aged and infirm; the uncertainties of agrarian life and daily struggles for sustenance; complex decisions about the use and dispositions of goods; the chaste exercise of sexual energy; responsibility for the earth; the discipline of education and study; proper care and exercise of the body through nutrition, diet, the balance of work and leisure; the tedium of too much work. Nothing escapes the constant coming of God. The contemplative is the one who sees this. Contemplation is a kind of knowledge of God "from the inside out," a kind of knowing God, not just knowing about God.

If he is an artist, a musician, a horticulturist, or a designer, everything he does is ordered to a deeper penetration of the mystery of loving relationship. The experience of union with God is to be found in a myriad of ways: affective, reflective, in the intellectual pursuit of truth, in the apprehension and pursuit of the good, in the simple appreciation of the beautiful. All forms of authentic human creativity, communication, and communion are potential avenues for union with the triune God.

True prayer, not the kind in which we sweetly rattle off an endless list of demands before God or endlessly agonize over meager conundrums, is a way of participating in communion with the living God. Our prayer penetrates to the heart of the Trinity when we live in such a way that the trinitarian life of God is disclosed in all our dealings with others. In the Trinity there is no domination and submission, no greater and lesser, no higher and lower among the three

persons. Father, Son, and Spirit exist in a relationship that is entirely mutual, reciprocal, and equal. Human relationships are iconic of the divine life. Or they can be.

Sin is the rupture of rightly ordered relationship with self, another, others, and God. It is the betrayal of the gift of the life of God within, a God whose very being is loving relation. And so there remains the need for constant forgiveness for our failure to be and become a living communion with the mystery of the living God.

In the whole of its liturgical life, but preeminently in the Eucharist, the monastic community enters into the deepest kind of communion with the whole church throughout the world, joined to it as members of Christ's Body. The sacred communion at the heart of the world includes the dead as well as all the living. The monk lives this mystery. It is all one. He lives in the presence of the communion of saints, those who have gone before us marked with the sign of faith. They are our forebears in faith and charity. Our beloved dead are our advocates. It is they who are living in glory. This cloud of witnesses surrounds the monk and his community as they move on the way to share in that glory: in the Spirit, through Christ, to the Father.

For the monk, as for all in the church, the Eucharist is the source and summit of the life of grace and Spirit. In the Eucharist, the monastic community expresses and receives its identity as the Body of Christ. As Christ's mysteries are celebrated in the eucharistic liturgy, the monastic community stands forth as members of Christ's Body, the church. The monastery is not an alternative church. The monastic life is not separate from the church's life and its concerns. Monastic living is life in the church. The monastery is a cell of the church whose members commit themselves to being and building the Body of Christ. The monastery is in the church, with the church, for the church.

This way of living is hidden in the recesses of the heart of the church, together with all those sick and suffering, persecuted and abandoned, wounded and weak, last and least—all those marginalized by society and by church, the unnoticed, the forgotten. Through the monks' prayer and constant supplication all are joined through the heart of Christ Crucified in the mystery of deep and abiding loving communion. They live with God in Christ. Hidden. As he lived. And lives even now.

Every human bond serves love's cause,
whether in the relationship of parents to children
or children to parents,
whether the deeper and closer relationship
of a husband to his wife
or a wife to her husband,
whether in any one of all the various relationships
that make up human society.
In all of these, love attracts them either to advance
or to strive to advance
toward a simple principle of unity.

John of Ford
Thirteenth-century Cistercian
On the Song of Songs

On Sacred Wednesday

The visitor:

> *What is the toughest thing*
> *about the monastic life?*

The monk:

> *It's not obedience.*
> *It's not celibacy.*
> *It's certainly not that we*
> *don't have our own bank*
> *accounts and credit cards.*
> *It's staying alive to it, doing*
> *the monastic thing day after*
> *day.*

The monk promises to stay in one place. He vows to love the brothers and the place in which he lives. The monastic vow of *conversatio morum* calls for an ongoing and lifelong commitment to a monastic way of living under a rule and an abbot. He also commits himself to stability, *stabilitas*. The monk pledges himself to the gift and task of conversion within the context of a specific community. He promises to live and die in one place, together with these brothers, unless sent to take part in a new monastic foundation. He does not move from place to place as the demands of some apostolic work such as preaching or teaching might require others to do. The monk is not a missionary moving about in service of the gospel. His "job"—indeed if a monk has a job at all—is to put roots down deeper and deeper in one monastery all of his days. If he moves to another monastery, more often than not he is sent by the abbot to respond to the needs of that monastic community. Then he stays there, stable in that place and loving those brothers.

By contrast, ours is a world of constant distraction and diversion. We race from one thing to the next, never really attentive to what is at hand, not really into what we are doing. We are hungry for experience; we want it all. And we are told that we can have it. It's all ours, if we make up our minds and work to make our dreams come true. Why settle for less?

Young families uproot themselves from their extended family and neighborhood in pursuit of a better job, more promising opportunities. "Bedroom communities" abound. Jobs are our new neighborhoods; shopping malls are our centers of community life. Indeed, the great medieval cathedral has been replaced by the mega-mall as the center of life and activity for many people today. Sunday afternoon is a time of relaxation—in front of the TV or shopping at the local mall. Every major city seems to claim that theirs is the biggest and the best. New, expanded, improved, "upgraded."

We live in an age of images. We are bombarded with messages. Quick information is at our fingertips. The television is our constant companion: one in the living room, each of the bedrooms, and often in the kitchen or the dining room. TV is on all the time, or most of it. "For companionship," many will say. Homes now have fax machines: sending a fax gives a subtle message that it's urgent. Fax back! Fast. Now, if you can—yesterday if it were possible. Now we can communicate with a whole world of total strangers without leaving home via e-mail and the Internet.

Restlessness is all-pervasive. We move through life in overdrive. The refrain is heard often enough these days: "Been there, done that." And we move on. Our yearning for constant diversion is unrelenting: more, bigger, louder. Even fine booksellers pump soft rock music into the ears of browsers. And dentists drill your teeth while you are being numbed by your favorite talk show host featuring "gangsta rap" music and endless "sista girl talk." Avoid feeling pain at all costs. Anything to take your mind off pain. And life. We live in a world of quick fix and sound bite. The result very often is that many of us are unable to give sustained attention to some of the fundamental realities of human life, let alone the mystery at the heart of it.

The monk, on the other hand, stays put, except for visits to the doctor and dentist. There may be other urgent matters that require his absence, but these are rare. For the most part the monk stays home. He makes a vow of stability: to stay in one place, one monastery, his whole life long. He does not wander. Although traveling monks are greeted warmly in whatever monastery they might visit, monks tend to be somewhat suspicious of brothers who wander away from home too much. Sinking down roots is at the heart of what it means to be a monk. Belonging to a house is what the life is about. This house, whichever one it might be.

Wednesday is "hump day" in the workaday world. Wednesday afternoon is just past the halfway mark. The bulk of the week is behind. But the anticipation of the weekend—"Thank God It's Friday"—is not yet in full bloom. On Wednesday afternoon there is often a mild fatigue in our bones. How much longer until week's end? Enthusiasm may have already been in short supply on Monday morning. Whatever energy may remain by Wednesday afternoon is nearing the bottom of the barrel, but we're not yet quite dried up. We are a bit low all right, but not running on empty. Not just yet.

On Wednesday afternoon there seems to be nothing much going on. It's the same old same old. This is the soil of a low grade depression, *acedia* in the language of monasticism. There is a listlessness in the land of the human heart. Ennui seems to be all-pervasive; there isn't much to hope for, to look forward to. It is the hour of the noonday devil. It is at this very point that we look for distraction. This is the moment when we crave diversion, anything to break out of the routine. In the ache of the ordinary, the monk's mind may wander, and he may wonder: Will there ever be just one Friday when it's not tomato soup and cheese sandwiches for supper? What's the point of this life? Why don't I *do* something with myself? How can I make a difference? Achieve something! Be productive! Make my mark on the world! Singing psalms seven times a day, every single day! Does that do anyone any good? Does it make any real difference?

On the face of it there is not much going on in the monastery—which is to say that something quite different goes on in the monastic life. There is no television. No radio. The daily paper is available in the

A young man seeking entrance to the monastery:

What do you do in the monastery?

Aelred Hagan
Novice Master
Mepkin Abbey:

Everything you will ever do here, you will have done in your first six months in the monastery.

We have scrambled eggs every day always the same way.

Aelred Hagan
Novice Master
Mepkin Abbey

On Sacred Wednesday

library, sometimes a day late. There are usually good periodical journals and magazines on the shelves. The monastery is a good place for people who are "addicted to print," those who love the written word, enjoy spending time with words, find bliss in the simple art of reading. Quietly. There is music for playing and for listening and plenty of acreage for long walks in the woods or a daily jog on the grounds. Or a lazy afternoon at the pond or by the river. Perhaps a morning off by the sea.

It is precisely in the midst of this, in this same old nothing-much-going-on, that the monk is to find the presence and action of God. Or let God find him. Monks are good at running too, just like all the rest of us. Some spend their whole lives finding ways to run in place. But staying alive to the monastic life entails finding the sacred not only in choir while chanting the psalms and in the celebration of the Eucharist and in the shared life of the brothers and in *lectio divina*, but even and especially when not much seems to be happening. In the doldrums. On Wednesday afternoon. Because often things are other than what they seem: the last shall be first, the least shall be the greatest; the seeds of the divine and the capacities of the human heart are found in weakness, not in strength. And every moment is shot through with God's abiding presence, even the doldrums of Wednesday afternoon. It too is to be kept holy, sacred, because something is indeed going on for those who know that there is more than meets the eye. We need to stand still long enough, stay in one place awhile, sink roots deep enough to see the sacred in Wednesday.

Though it may appear otherwise, there is not much that is really extraordinary about the monastic life, especially after the novelty wears off and the grind of the routine sets in. The monk is called to the same holiness as everyone baptized into the Body of Christ. This holiness rests in the flourishing of charity. Whatever there may be by way of the extraordinary lies in the stick-with-it-ness of the monk. His life is ordered in such a way that he might resist the distractions and diversions, cacophony and clutter that most of us allow to have the upper hand in our lives. The monastic life provides occasion to lean toward the presence of God even and especially on Wednesday afternoon—in the altogether ordinary, daily, boring routine that makes up a large part of our lives.

In many ways, the monk's life is quite ordinary and unexciting: waking up and washing up, dressing and preparing for work, standing alongside others doing chores he'd rather were someone else's to do, caring for others living under his roof and beyond it, growing old and hopefully dying gracefully. It is not his task to do any great work. His call is to grow in the grace of being conformed to the person of Christ with these brothers and in this place. He lives a hidden life. He and his brothers live outside the limelight. The monk is at the margins of society. He knows that the longest journey is the journey inward to discover the true self, the self conformed to the person of Christ and united with God and others. But such a journey is not a free and easy ride. How much easier life would be if there were just a little excitement, a little something to take the mind off it all. Perhaps a drink? Just one! Or a vacation? Just one long weekend! Some would settle for a half gallon of ice cream, any flavor. Just a little diversion. Something. Anything.

The monk's call is the same one, more or less, sounded in the heart of each of us. But we rarely hear it for the sound of our own wheels spinning away at constant diversion and distraction. No matter what our walk of life, it is ours to listen deeply, to tend to the tasks that have been given to us, to care for those near, to recognize and respect the dignity and value of the other. But what is hardest of all is to accept the

fact that the lot of a great number of us is to do very small things. Our great vocation is to do small and seemingly insignificant things with great love.

So many of us are inclined to imagine that we are destined for big things, and so our lives seem to us one big disappointment. We live in a prolonged state of disillusionment. We might even get lost in fantasy: Perhaps I'll join a monastery! A great life indeed. Heroic. But it is a life never greater or more adventuresome or self-sacrificing than on Wednesday afternoon. Each Wednesday. Every single Wednesday. Wednesday after Wednesday when nothing, absolutely nothing, seems to be happening.

Between Darkness and Light

If I say, "Surely the darkness shall cover me,
and the light around me become night,"
even the darkness is not dark to you;
the night is as bright as the day,
for darkness is as light to you.

Psalm 139

The human heart is a region of great light. And of profound darkness. It is that place in us where the struggle between good and evil takes place. The battle is constant. It does not end until we draw our last breath. Even when we are nearing our final hour, there is a choice. We can decide to surrender into the hands of the benevolent and trustworthy Source and Sustainer of all life or to grip and cling to what we have and what we know. Choosing life often means surrendering to the unknown, the uncertain, the unfathomable. It means giving in to the Other. It means welcoming the darkness of which is born light and life and love.

But not all darkness is a friend. Much of it is to be resisted, and it is not always easy to resist. Hence the need for discernment, sorting out the good from all the rest. And developing a discerning heart takes rigorous discipline. Not all that passes for good is in fact so. Not everything that we think is true is the truth, no matter how deeply we may feel that it is. And not all the values that we think valuable are worth holding on to. Sifting out the spiritual from the nonspiritual and the unspiritual takes effort. It is work. And it requires the assistance of others more attuned to the ways of the Spirit than we are.

Self-scrutiny and self-examination are necessary ingredients in the spiritual life. We always run the risk of living an illusion. Christian life is not a smooth, easy ride. Those who see it as such may in fact be living in the land of illusion. In our own day the spiritual life is often spoken of in terms of self-fulfillment and self-actualization. Spiritual disciplines are thought to make things easier, increase productivity, help one go through life with a sort of unflappable serenity. They may indeed. But in themselves these are not good reasons to embark on the path of the Christian spiritual life. The Christian undertakes a serious pursuit of the spiritual life for one reason—to live in Christ, to be conformed to the person of Christ.

The Cross of Christ is the vital center for all reflection and discernment in the Christian life. The Cross is the centerpiece of all Christian spirituality. It is the gauge for judging authentic spiritual growth and development, a means of separating wheat from chaff. Talk of spirituality may sound light and airy, even fluffy. It may seem fuzzy unless and until the Word of the Cross is discerned as the Word beneath the words.

Living in the shadow of the Cross with nothing except the simple hope of new life promised in the Resurrection is the mark of the mature Christian. The Cross serves as a constant reminder that the forces of evil, and our tendency to give in to them, are quite real. There are negative forces in the world and in us and in those we love as well as in our enemies. Evil and sin do not disappear if we pretend they do not exist or if we insist that people are good or nice or sweet. The negative factors of human existence cannot be bypassed on the superhighway of spirituality with its signposts pointing the way toward self-fulfillment and prosperity.

Christian spirituality is rooted in the Paschal Mystery of Christ. Those who follow him are marked with the sign of the Cross. This means that the way to life and light and love is in and through diminishment, darkness, and death—not around it. There are no shortcuts. There is no bypass.

The Christian life rests on the conviction that evil and sin are real forces in the world and that these powers cannot be ignored. Self-absorption, self-fixation, self-preoccupation all give ample evidence of their presence. Senseless violence, the slaughter of innocent millions, the age-old conflicts of warring nations, races, and classes all give the lie to the claim that people are entirely good and that there is no such thing as evil or sin. Any serious engagement with the Christian spiritual life yields a crucial insight early on: Being nice is not necessarily being good. Making good on life and life's promises is both gift and task. It involves living between the darkness and the light, struggling with the powers of evil and sin, and counting on the constancy of grace and mercy for the many times in a day and over the course of a lifetime when we simply give in to the sway and the slumber of the dark.

Light and good and truth and beauty are constantly assaulted. At every turn they are defiled. By us. Light is dimmed, goodness and truth betrayed, beauty disfigured. Their vestiges remain, but they must be searched for and found. And they can be found only by those willing to go the extra mile, those who are willing to pay the price. The cost is high because the threats against them are so constant, rendering them all the more precious. The monk pays the price with a life—his own life, whole and entire. His constant quest is for integration in human life, the world, the church, in light of forces of suffering, disintegration, and depersonalization brought on by evil and sin.

The monk is a marginal person. He lives at the margins of society and even of the church, at least so it seems. He lives at the edge of the mainstream. He does not engage in the struggles that most people face: for a better job, a bigger house, a better education for the children. There are other struggles that may seem far less noble. Very often unconscious, they are far more problematic: the struggle for more recognition, for higher achievements, for a little revenge for the hurt that has been inflicted on me or on those I love. There is always a reason for revenge, no? This is closer to the monk's constant struggle. Because his field is the human heart.

Here the monk does not stand on the sidelines. The heart is the monk's turf. It is his métier. His permanent place is between the

darkness and the light of the human heart, this region of wound and wisdom, this land called desire. He stands. So steadfastly does he stand there, between the darkness and the light, that what once seemed marginal to the human story can now be seen as its center. For there is nothing more central to the task of being and becoming human than the full flourishing of the heart's yearning. And the monk is at the very center of bringing that to be, allowing it to stand forth in all its fullness.

The heart longs to be in relation with another, others, God. But there are blocks, obstacles, dark spots. We can't just glide past them. There is danger, and it is quite real. Even the very best of human relationships have an inherently dark side, and so does our relationship to God. The experience of God is not all sweetness and light. Because of the darkness, the experience of God's hiddenness and absence, many shy away. They seek protection from it. They do not keep on the path. They quit. It's too troubling. It is simply too painful to go on praying when there seems to be no answer, no one listening.

It is not only in the light that the presence of God is known. It is also the piercing, agonizing darkness, the silence that yields a knowledge of God's presence. By unknowing. A host of witnesses, mystics, and teachers of the spiritual life serve to remind us: If you have known, then what you have known is not God. At least not the fullness of God. If you want to be sure of the road you are on you must close your eyes and keep walking in the dark.

But this darkness dazzles. In God there is no darkness at all. Darkness is pierced, not always with light but with promise. Because of God's promise, the night and the day are both alike. In tasting the absence, we long for God's presence. We search, seek, strain, look for clues, for traces—the traces that God puts into us—so that we might follow. But there sometimes seems to be no way and nowhere to go.

Often we have to make a way where there has been none before. This we do by believing in God's promise, which is given as we stand between the darkness and the light, trusting in the light even and especially in the darkest night.

Lingering long enough in vigil, in *lectio*, in quiet, resisting restlessness and diversion, the monk tries to come to terms with darkness as a permanent factor of human existence. His existence. The dark becomes familiar. He makes his home there in the darkness. He sees that darkness is the terrain of every human heart. He recognizes that place whenever he encounters another. There are shadows everywhere. The struggle is always apparent to him—in the beleaguered gait of a guest, in the snide remarks of a brother in the community, in the languishing of a life once so promising, in the news of an unbreakable addiction gripping his niece or his cousin. This is his terrain. It is never someone else's issue entirely or someone else's problem to handle alone, or the other person's cross to take up and bear. It is his. He lives now with Christ: crucified, died, buried. The Christ who descended, went down, deep down: unto death and into hell. There he lives, with all the nameless, forgotten, abandoned, scorned. With Christ. In those depths. Standing. In the darkness. Into the unfathomable bottoms of the human heart. Abandoned even by God?

Christ is there: unto death and into hell, joining all the living and the dead in one immutable act of love. Sinners and saints. Christ lives in each one. Between darkness and light, there is life. Even in utter darkness there is life, for Christ is there. He is life. And life is this—to lay down one's life for another. Crucified love: unto death and into hell. The hell of the heart is the very soil of hope, for God is there. Even and especially there, in the sorrow of the human heart: bruised, broken, crushed, betrayed. Abandoned even by God? Whisper, just one word, and even the ones caught in the hell of their own making may hear the stirrings of hope. In no other place is it more nobly born than in the hell of our own hearts. The deep-down, lasting kind of hope, born in the darkness of the human heart.

Not only is our light full of darkness,
  the darkness grows with the light.
"The Lord is light and no darkness can find any place in him,"
  yet his unapproachable light itself produces our darkness.
Two things, you see, cause darkness:
  insufficient light and over-abundant light.
Light's own source says, "Turn your eyes away,
  they compel me to depart."
"Lord, you have kept my lamp alight till now;
  dispel, I pray, this darkness of mine."

Isaac of Stella
Twelfth-century Cistercian
A Fifth Sermon for Sexagesima

Waiting

Wait, my soul, silent for God,
for God alone, my hope,
alone my rock, my safety,
my refuge: I stand secure.

Psalm 62

If we hope for something we do not see, then we exercise patience in waiting.

Guerric of Igny
Twelfth-century Cistercian
The First Sermon for Advent

There is nothing worse than waiting. What a nuisance! A waste of precious time. On edge for days until the results of the doctor's tests are in. The flight is delayed, after all are on board. Hours on the runway before taking off. Standing at the bus stop in the rain. Eighth in the express checkout lane at the grocery, the car is double-parked, and the person next in line pulls out a checkbook after the groceries have been rung up and then asks: "What's the name of this store?" The best restaurant in town, and the waiter hasn't a clue what "we're really pressed for time" means. Looking forward to those two weeks of vacation that never get here. And whether that letter is a word of acceptance or rejection is up for grabs. It could go either way. Hate waiting. Yes or no. If only we knew for sure one way or the other.

What many of us detest, the monk spends a lifetime doing. He waits for the God who comes sometimes in a moment of dazzling darkness but more often over the long haul of waiting things out. For the whole of a life.

The monk is single, celibate, in itself a sign of incompletion, of something yet to be fulfilled. He is a witness to something more. There are regular fasts. The empty stomach aches to be filled, the body to be nourished. Running on empty requires looking to another for steam, for energy. He cannot go it alone. He must look for the other. Wait for something beyond himself. Famished for the Word of God. So hungry he could almost eat the pages of the book. The very point indeed.

He rises long before dawn while others take their rest, so that he might keep vigil. Vigilance is anticipation. Keeping watch. Looking. Expecting. Staying ready. Longing for that which is not yet here. Counting on the rising of the sun. Hoping for the coming of the light. Waiting for daybreak.

It is not just in the darkness of the night that the monk waits. Expectation is his path, his posture, his position in life. He is not his own agent. He is not self-sufficient. He looks to others: the wisdom of brothers, the teaching of the abbot, the needs of the church, the beauty of the liturgy, the rhythms of the seasons and the saints. He waits for the guests to be served before beginning to eat. He waits for the brothers to gather for prayer. He waits for the cheese to ripen before wrapping and the herbs to dry before packing.

There are hints everywhere. He listens. Tunes his ear. Squints to catch a glimpse. Rays of light abound. It might be light-years away from him, but come it does. It might be days before the echo of the Word reaches his ear and offers some small consolation, and he must bear the burden of waiting. He must endure until it reaches him. He need only stand still. Be open. Stay in one place. It will come. It always does, like an answer to a prayer just when he is on the verge of giving up. It comes just in time. Sure as day's dawn. He knows that waiting is the better part of wisdom. He's learned it by waiting long enough to know. The hard way. The only way for him. The way of a monk.

We want it now. All of it. Whatever it might be. Results. Plans realized. Goals achieved. Dreams come true. Supper on the table. Language mastered. Skills acquired. An answer to that letter. Or fax. And we want our prayers answered, too. If there is no answer to our prayers, then why bother with God? What's the point? If God is not useful, if God does not help us out, then why waste our time and energy?

The monk waits for God even when prayers seem to go unheard and unanswered. He keeps standing in one place. His place. This place. He is a lover of the brothers and of the place. He answered God's call to be in this place simply because God is God, and this is God's place. The monk lives by the promise of presence. The presence is known deep inside him from time to time. But mostly he goes from hunch to hunch, hint after hint, by the whisper of a promise. He has staked his life on it and continues to do so day by day in lifelong fidelity. Will he make good on his own promise given in a whisper of fidelity? He waits to see. And he keeps walking, seeking the face of God, and counting on grace.

The God who is God for us is at one and the same time at hand and always yet to come. The divine grace and presence overspill our tightly knit concepts and categories. God is always ahead and ever more than we can ask or imagine. We want to pin it down, tie it down, be certain of God's nearness. The monk leans into a grace loose in the world, searching for traces. Nothing is quite large enough for the abundance of God's gracious mercy—not his own life, the monastery, or even the church. He is willing to wait for God's word of mercy—just one word—his whole life long. Waiting while walking. Making a way where there has been none before. Preparing. For the coming of God.

He waits in silence and in solitude alongside his brothers, yet also in the presence of another. Mary. They draw near her in the darkness. The woman who waits, the mother who prays, the icon of the contemplative. She does not clutch or cling. It is they who cling to her with their words: "O clement, O loving, O sweet Virgin Mary." She is tender, and she is strong. She is a woman of courage and of faith. She who listened long and lovingly, perplexed and puzzled, was yet poised in freedom of spirit. Just as he is now at the close of day as he greets this woman of the dark. The darkness is the very soil of hope. From it the light springs. In the beginning it was all there was. And God was there, even in the darkness.

She waits with him there, for him, there in the darkness. In his sleep. The Word is within him, breathing through the Spirit, even as he sleeps. She waits until he rises when he will wait yet again for the

God who comes. She is Mother of God and his mother. Open. Expecting. Anticipating the Word become flesh of her life. And his. But he must wait as she did, so that his life too might be overshadowed by the Spirit of God and the Word become flesh through his tired yet hopeful flesh and bones.

His life seems one of endless waiting. Even at the end of his life he waits. Yes, especially then, he waits. He waits in quiet prayer alongside other brothers who together with him have spent their lives waiting, expecting the God who is now soon to come: "How long, O Lord? How long? Take what little remains—a heart purified by vigil, by fast, by living singly and by searching solitude, by giving shape to a space widened by a whole way of life so that You could find a home in this broken and spent self. Come. Take. Receive."

Nothing is more central, more crucial to being human than hope. And hope looks to a future good not yet in hand. We must wait because hope looks to a future possibility that can only come as gift. We may live without faith. Many do. And we can go through life, even succeed, without loving or being loved. The evidence abounds, as do the sad consequences. But without hope we do not live. Without it we cannot go on. Hope is that which takes the next step, based on two intuitions that seem to be saying different things. Hope sees that something is quite difficult, hard to attain, out of reach. But hope also sees that it's worth striving for because hope knows that, hard as something might be, it is still possible. Hope is hospitality to challenge. Hope is a reach. It buoys up and carries to the future.

No matter how uncertain the future might be, hope keeps moving toward it. Hope simply takes the next step. Hope turns the page. Hope looks to a gift still on offer. Not to this thing or that one. Not to a dream come true. The deep-down hope by which we live spurs us on

beyond this or that thing we hope for. It waits, long and lovingly—for more. For life. For tomorrow. For future. Beyond these wishes and those wants. For that which is not apparent. Beyond all that meets the eye. Hope hopes to keep on hoping, waiting for the gift of God's constant coming. Nothing more. Or less. God. Come.

The monastic vocation is therefore by its very nature a call to the wilderness, because it is a call to live in hope. The monk carries on the long tradition of waiting and hoping.

Thomas Merton
Twentieth-century Cistercian
Silence in Heaven

Order of Cistercians of the Strict Observance
United States Region
Arranged by filiation and date of foundation

Men's Houses

Abbey of Gethsemani
(Founded from Melleray, France, in 1848)
3642 Monks Road
Trappist, KY 40051-6102
Phone (502) 549-3117
Fax   (502) 549-4124

Monastery of the Holy Spirit
(Founded from Gethsemani in 1944)
2625 Highway 212 S. W.
Conyers, GA 30208-4044
Phone (770) 483-8705
Fax   (770) 760-0989

Abbey of the Holy Trinity
(Founded from Gethsemani in 1947)
1250 South 9500 East
Huntsville, UT 84317
Phone (801) 745-3784
Fax   (801) 745-6430

Mepkin Abbey
(Founded from Gethsemani in 1949)
1098 Mepkin Abbey Road
Moncks Corner, SC 29461-4796
Phone (803) 761-8509
Fax   (803) 761-6719
WEB   http://www.mepkinabbey.org

Our Lady of the Genesee Abbey
(Founded from Gethsemani in 1951)
PO Box 900
Piffard, NY 14533-0900
Phone (716) 243-0660
Fax   (716) 243-4816

Our Lady of New Clairvaux Abbey
(Founded from Gethsemani in 1955)
7th and C Streets
PO Box 80
Vina, CA 96092-0080
Phone (916) 839-2161
Fax   (916) 839-2332

New Melleray Abbey
(Founded from Mount Melleray, Ireland, in 1849)
6500 Melleray Circle
Peosta, IA 52068
Phone (319) 588-2319
Fax   (319) 588-4117

Assumption Abbey
(Founded from New Melleray in 1951)
Route 5, Box 1056
Ava, MO 65608-9120
Phone (417) 683-5110
Fax   (417) 683-5658

Women's Houses

St. Joseph's Abbey
(Originally founded in Canada in 1868)
Spencer, MA 01562-1233
Phone (508) 885-8700
Fax   (508) 885-8701

Mount St. Mary's Abbey
(Founded from Glencairn, Ireland, in 1949)
300 Arnold Street
Wrentham, MA 02093
Phone (508) 528-1282
Fax   (508) 528-5360

Our Lady of Guadalupe Abbey
(Founded from Spencer in 1948)
Box 97
Lafayette, OR 97127
Phone (503) 852-7174
Fax   (503) 852-7748

Our Lady of the Mississippi Abbey
(Founded from Wrentham in 1964)
8400 Abbey Hill Road
Dubuque, IA 52003-9501
Phone (319) 582-2595
Fax   (319) 582-5511

Holy Cross Abbey
(Founded from Spencer in 1950)
Route Two—Box 3870
Berryville, VA 22611-9526
Phone (540) 955-1425
Fax   (540) 955-1356

Santa Rita Abbey
(Founded from Wrentham in 1972)
HC 1 Box 929
Sonoita, AZ 85637-9705
Phone (520) 455-5595
Fax   (520) 455-5770

Saint Benedict's Abbey
(Founded from Spencer in 1956)
1012 Monastery Road
Snowmass, CO 81654-9399
Phone (970) 927-3311
Fax   (970) 927-3399

Our Lady of the Angels Monastery
(Founded from Wrentham in 1987)
3365 Monastery Drive
Crozet, VA 22932-9802
Phone (804) 823-1452
Fax   (804) 823-6379

Redwoods Monastery
(Founded from Nazareth, Belgium, in 1962)
18104 Briceland Thorn Road
Whitethorn, CA 95589
Phone (707) 986-7419
Fax   (707) 986-7419

Order of Cistercians of the Strict Observance

Canadian Region
Arranged by filiation and date of foundation

Men's Houses

Abbaye cistercienne N.-D. du Lac

(Founded from Bellefontaine, France, in 1881)
1600 Chemin d'Oka
Oka, Québec, J0N 1E0
Canada
Phone (514) 479-8361
Fax   (514) 479-8364

Abbaye cistercienne

(Founded from Oka in 1892)
100, Route des Trappistes
Mistassini, Québec, G8M 3B2
Canada
Phone (418) 276-0491
Fax   (418) 276-8885

Cistercian Monastery of Notre Dame

(Founded from Oka in 1977)
R.R. No. 5
Orangeville, Ontario, L9W 2Z2
Canada
Phone (519) 941-9428
Fax   (519) 941-6510

Abbaye cistercienne N.-D. des Prairies

(Founded from Bellefontaine, France, in 1892)
C.P. 310
Holland, Manitoba, R0G 0X0
Canada
Phone (204) 526-2000
Fax   (204) 526-2002

Abbaye N.-D. du Calvaire

(Founded from Bonnecombe, France, in 1902)
R.R. 3, Boîte 25
Rogersville, N. Br., E0A 2T0
Canada
Phone (506) 775-2331
Fax   (506) 775-6220

Women's Houses

Abbaye N.-D. de L'Assomption
(Founded from Vaisse, France, in 1818)
C.P. 119
Rogersville, N. B. E0A 2T0
Canada
Phone (506) 775-2322
Fax   (506) 775-6295

Abbaye cistercienne Saint-Romuald
(Founded from Bonnevalle, France, in 1902)
C.P. 3999 Terminus Lévis
Lévis, Québec, G6V 6V4
Canada
Phone (418) 839-9993
Fax   (418) 839-0675

For Further Reading

Sources

Aelred of Rievaulx. *Mirror of Charity*. Cistercian Fathers 17. Kalamazoo,
MI: Cistercian Publications, 1990.

———. *Spiritual Friendship*. Cistercian Fathers 5. Washington, DC:
Cistercian Publications, 1974.

Bernard of Clairvaux. *On Loving God*. Cistercian Fathers 13B. Kalamazoo,
MI: Cistercian Publications, 1994.

———. *On the Song of Songs* I-IV. Kalamazoo, MI: Cistercian Publications,
1971-1980.

Guerric of Igny. *The Liturgical Sermons* I. Cistercian Fathers 8. Spencer,
MA: Cistercian Publications, 1971.

———. *The Liturgical Sermons* II. Cistercian Fathers 32. Spencer, MA:
Cistercian Publications, 1971.

Isaac of Stella. *Sermons on the Christian Year*. Cistercian Fathers 11.
Kalamazoo, MI: Cistercian Publications, 1979.

The Letters of Armand-Jean de Rancé, Abbot and Reformer of La Trappe.
Edited and translated by Alban J. Krailsheimer. Cistercian Studies 80, 81.
Kalamazoo, MI: Cistercian Publications, 1984.

The Rule of St. Benedict (RB 1980). Edited by Timothy Fry. Collegeville,
MN: Liturgical Press, 1981.

Waddell, Helen, trans. *The Desert Fathers*. New York: Sheed & Ward, 1936.

Ward, Benedicta, trans. *The Sayings of the Desert Fathers*. Cistercian
Studies 59. Kalamazoo, MI: Cistercian Publications, 1975.

William of Saint Thierry. *The Golden Epistle: A Letter to the Brethren at Mont Dieu*. Cistercian Fathers 12. Spencer, MA: Cistercian Publications, 1971.

———. *On Contemplating God; Prayer; Meditations*. Cistercian Fathers 3. Kalamazoo, MI: Cistercian Publications, 1977.

Contemporary Writings

Altermatt, Alberic. "The Cistercian Patrimony: An Introduction to the Most Important Historical, Juridical and Spiritual Documents." *Cistercian Studies Quarterly* 25 (1990): 287-328.

Bouyer, Louis. *The Cistercian Heritage*. Westminster, MD: Newman Press, 1958.

Casey, Michael. *Athirst for God: Spiritual Desire in Bernard of Clairvaux's Sermon on the Song of Songs*. Cistercian Studies 77. Kalamazoo, MI: Cistercian Publications, 1988.

———. *Sacred Reading: The Ancient Art of Lectio Divina*. Liguori, MO: Triumph Books, 1995.

———. *Toward God: The Ancient Wisdom of Western Prayer*. Liguori, MO: Triumph Books, 1995.

Cummings, Charles. *Monastic Practices*. Cistercian Studies 75. Kalamazoo, MI: Cistercian Publications, 1986.

de Vogüé, Adalbert. *Reading Saint Benedict*. Cistercian Studies 151. Kalamazoo, MI: Cistercian Publications, 1994.

Kelty, Matthew. *Aspects of the Monastic Calling*. Trappist, KY: Abbey of Gethsemani, 1975.

Kline, Francis. *Lovers of the Place: Monasticism Loose in the Church.* Collegeville, MN: Liturgical Press, 1997.

Knowles, David. *Christian Monasticism.* World University Library. New York: McGraw-Hill, 1969.

Leclercq, Jean. *Bernard of Clairvaux and the Cistercian Spirit.* Cistercian Studies 16. Kalamazoo, MI: Cistercian Publications, 1976.

———. *The Love of Learning and the Desire for God: A Study of Monastic Culture.* New York: Fordham University Press, 1961.

Lekai, Louis. *The Cistercians: Ideals and Reality.* Kent, OH: Kent State University Press, 1977.

Louf, André. *The Cistercian Way.* Cistercian Studies 96. Kalamazoo, MI: Cistercian Publications, 1983.

———. *Teach Us to Pray: Learning a Little About God.* Chicago: Franciscan Herald Press, 1975.

McGinn, Bernard. *The Growth of Mysticism: Gregory the Great Through the Twelfth Century.* New York: Crossroad, 1994.

Merton, Thomas. *The Monastic Journey.* Edited by Patrick Hart. Cistercian Studies 133. Kalamazoo, MI: Cistercian Publications, 1992.

———. *Silence in Heaven: A Book of the Monastic Life.* New York: Thomas Crowell, 1956.

———. *The Waters of Siloe.* New York: Harcourt, Brace, 1949.

Pennington, M. Basil, ed. *The Cistercian Spirit: A Symposium.* Cistercian Studies 3. Shannon: Irish University Press, 1970.